Red Brother, White Brother

A TIME FOR ATONEMENT

"At-one-ment – to be of one mind"

By Dr. Jean Lafrance

iUniverse, Inc.
Bloomington

RED BROTHER, WHITE BROTHER
A TIME FOR ATONEMENT

iUniverse books may be ordered through booksellers or by contacting:

iUniverse
1663 Liberty Drive
Bloomington, IN 47403
www.iuniverse.com
1-800-Authors (1-800-288-4677)

ISBN: 978-1-4759-6834-7 (sc)
ISBN: 978-1-4759-6835-4 (ebk)

Library of Congress Control Number: 2012924183

Printed in the United States of America

iUniverse rev. date: 1/10/2013

Red Brother, White Brother

Contents

PART II: THE EXPERIENCE OF ABORIGINAL PEOPLE WITH CHILD WELFARE

PART III: ABORIGINAL WORLD VIEWS AND THE ADMINISTRATIVE STATE

PART IV: MERGING THE EXPERIENCE OF ABORIGINAL PEOPLE WITH PROGRAM AND POLICY CHANGE

Within the ancient Hopi Indian Prophecy is told the history of the Red and White brothers, sons of the Earth Mother and the Great Spirit who gave them different missions. The Red Brother was to stay at home and keep the land in sacred trust while the White Brother went abroad to record things and make inventions. One day the White Brother was to return and share his inventions in a spirit of respect for the wisdom his Red Brother had gained. It was told that his inventions would include cobwebs through which people could speak to each other from house to house across mountains, even with all doors and windows closed; there would be carriages crossing the sky on invisible roads, and eventually a gourd of ashes that when dropped would scorch the earth and even the fishes in the sea. If the White Brother's ego grew so large in making these inventions that he would not listen to the wisdom of the Red Brother, he would bring this world to an end in the Great purification of nature. Only a few would survive to bring forth the next world in which there would again be abundance and harmony.

The most promising survival path for humans is to merge existing technology with the knowledge, wisdom, and ecologically sound practice of indigenous and traditional peoples ~ (Sahtouris, 1992, p.1).

AT-ONE-MENT

Derived from the Latin words *Adunare* and *Reconciliatio*

Adunare (v.) Latin. def.
To unite, make as one

Reconciliatio (n.) Latin. def.
To bring together again, to restore to union

Acknowledgements

This book is the culmination of nearly a half century of active work with child welfare as a practitioner, administrator, executive leader, child advocate, teacher and researcher. I owe everything to the people with whom I crossed paths during that time. I cannot possibly mention them all, but here are some of them.

I wish to thank my Dean in the Faculty of Social Work, Gayla Rogers, and Nancy Reynolds, President and Chief Executive Officer of the Alberta Center for Child, Family and Community Research for their collaboration in providing me with the time to develop the monograph that morphed into this book. I am especially grateful for their patience as I grappled with the many challenges that it presented.

My thanks for my youngest daughter, Kristine Morris, who editorial support has given my words greater elegance than they deserve.

I wish to acknowledge to following groups and persons who have attempted to teach me on this journey of understanding. After 46 years of working with Aboriginal people in many parts of Alberta, and having been raised in St. Paul where my earliest memories are of the Aboriginal people from surrounding reserves camping near our home, I cannot possibly acknowledge all of the people who have helped me.

My thanks to my Aboriginal clients, from when I was a caseworker in St. Paul to the families I encountered in Bonnyville, Lethbridge, Wetaskiwin, Edmonton and Calgary. They have taught me so much about courage in the face of challenges, humanity in the face of inhumanity and generosity of spirit in the face of immense difficulties. Some have become powerful allies in my work with their families, where I learned that they could be a force for change within their communities.

To my friends at Sturgeon Lake who shared their stories about the residential school experiences and who worked on developing a renewed community vision. Allowing me to participate in their Journey toward Empowerment will always have a special place in my heart. Their continued role in *Making our Hearts Sing* has inspired me with their patience and persistence in the face of the many obstacles placed in their path.

I wish to acknowledge the following persons from the Blood Reserve who did yeoman work in arranging and facilitating our consultations with their Tribal members: Betty Bastien, Susan Bare Shin Bone, Robin Little Bear, Kim Gravelle and Lance Tailfeathers along with many other staff who were expert in the use of the open space concept that formed the basis for *Making our Hearts Sing*. From Sturgeon Lake David Nabew, Leroy Hamelin, and Alvina Nabew were constant in their support and willingness to offer hospitality on many occasions such as our gathering on "Creating Hope." From the Métis Child and Family Services Region of ACYS: Shane Gauthier, Shannon Souray and Lillian Parenteau must also be acknowledged.

A special thanks to the hundreds of community members who contributed to this work. It is difficult to pick some as they are too numerous, but I would be remiss if I did not mention

Rosie Day Rider, Nina Scout and Andy Blackwater from the Blood Tribe, as well as Mary Kappo, Margaret Kappo, and Jerry Goodswimmer from Sturgeon Lake for their friendship and support.

I wish to acknowledge my colleagues Betty Bastien, Ralph Bodor and William Pelech, who collaborated in the production of the monograph upon which one of the chapters is based. It is entitled *Leadership Forums in Aboriginal Child welfare: Making our Hearts Sing* and is available on line on the Center of Excellence for Child welfare at http://www.cecw-cepb.ca/catalogue.

I am grateful to the 80 persons who joined our gathering at Nakoda Lodge where the communities of the Blood Tribe (Kainai Nation), the Sturgeon Lake Cree Nation, and the Métis Settlements shared their vision for the future at the *Making our Hearts Sing* gathering. During a 2-day session in this deeply spiritual place, these communities came up with nearly 600 concrete ideas on how to change child welfare systems to conform to their vision. I consider myself blessed by their wisdom and creativity. My thanks to Robin Little Bear and Lance Tailfeathers for leading the group through an open space process that allowed this this knowledge to emerge.

Thank you to The Bent Arrow Traditional Healing Society and the Energy Square Neighborhood Center for providing an opportunity to dialogue with their staff for over a year. I wish to especially acknowledge Shauna Seneca, with whom we began this journey, and who sadly passed away just prior to beginning this initiative. Cheryl Whiskeyjack was pressed into service as Executive Director, and not only did she graciously support our efforts, she participated in all of our sessions with Bent Arrow and government staff. We wish to thank the nine staff who took time from their busy lives to reflect on a monthly basis on their work and the context in which it was performed.

I am grateful for the children who were on my caseload as a social worker in St. Paul and who have come back into my life. Much time has passed and we are now all grandparents. I am saddened by the horrific experiences that they have undergone during their time in child welfare, and sobered by their accounts of their lives; they have so much to teach us. I wish I could say that such events no longer take place, but they do. Our reconnection is bittersweet: tinged with regret yet inspired by their courage in ensuring that none of their children will repeat their experiences: Sharon, Martha, Herb, Eugene, Clifford, Barbara, Lillian, and Percy—you know who you are. Thank you for coming back into my life.

To the 160 persons who spent their childhood in child welfare system and came together to share their testimonials; these were powerful and motivating and can help to improve our services based upon your life experience. While this short summary cannot do justice to the pathos and pain that you have experienced, I applaud your courage and willingness to share with each other and support one another. Thank you also to the child welfare staff who joined us in hearing your stories. Your support was invaluable to all of us.

To the Aboriginal students that I have taught in Edmonton, Hobbema, Blue Quills, and Red Crow—thank you. You give me hope for the future. My prayer is that your passion for social work and your commitment to your people will be nurtured and supported as you grow into what you could be. You have taught me as much as I have taught you, and this work has been influenced by you more than you could know. You have confirmed my belief that Aboriginal people know exactly what to do to fulfill their vision.

To my colleagues with the Prairie Child welfare Consortium in the Prairie Provinces: You have been a source of constant support and inspiration. Our bi-annual symposia are an essential part of my renewal as hundreds of Aboriginal people come together with academics, government and their peers to share their knowledge on issues of great importance to children and families. May our Consortium live long and prosper!

To Sarah Potts, with whom I have reunited after 40 years—still the 19 year old firebrand who initiated so many innovations during my time in Wetaskiwin. After so many years, we continue to share the same hopes and aspirations.

I want to express my appreciation for the support that Bernadette Iahtail, Co-founder and Executive Director of the Creating Hope Society, who has become an important ally and a good friend with whom I share a common vision—An Aboriginal home for ever Aboriginal child by 2025.

And most of all, my dear Marie-Anna, who has shared this sometimes tumultuous journey every step of the way, and who asks me from time to time—*What has really changed since we began, Jean. I keep hearing of the same things over and over again.* I sense that windows are opening to let in the sunshine of illumination and a fresh breeze that will blow the dusty remnants of useless practices, leaving our Aboriginal friends with a clean slate upon which to build.

PART I

Laying the groundwork

Introduction

The Hopi Prophecy at the start of the book tells of the separate journeys of the Red brother and the White brother in their search of knowledge. The story cautions that if the White brother's ego grew too large while on his journey, he would be unwilling to listen to the wisdom and knowledge gained by the Red brother while they were apart. The point of the prophecy is that a merging of knowledge, a mutual sense of respect for the other's ways of knowing is essential for ultimate survival.

The parallels between this story and the present day state of Aboriginal child welfare are overwhelming. From the time of colonization when children were separated from their communities for the purpose of taking the "Indian" out of them, to modern day child welfare practices, the common denominator is that the "White brother" is still not listening to his "Red brother." Regardless of the plethora of research and scholarly articles outlining the issues within the system, clearly delineating what is missing, what is needed and what is wrong. Regardless of the many Aboriginal communities who have, separately or collectively, raised their voices and let their needs be known, along with thoughtful solutions to the issues. Regardless of all the evidence pointing to the fact that the current Aboriginal child welfare system *is not working.*

The numbers of Aboriginal children being removed from their families and communities continues to grow; this continuous and cumulative loss within the communities is staggering, and only serves to perpetuate the ongoing trauma and its ill effects. There is a saying, "Insanity is doing the same thing, over and over again, but expecting different results." Why, then, would it seem viable to continue imposing the same policies and practices in Aboriginal child welfare over and over again, given the negative outcomes? Why, then, do people continue to be shocked when they find that the system does not work? Instead of throwing money into more research to define who is responsible for what or to further define what the communities need and what the vision is, pay attention to what has already been shared. The communities have painstakingly repeated their needs, their suggestions for change, and their desire for autonomy in creating this change. It's time to listen—really listen—to respect that the answers lie within the people.

The time for atonement is upon us; the time for government officials, policy makers and child welfare agencies to open their minds and hearts to restoring the union of the Red brother and the White brother, accepting and respecting the different ways of knowing and, together, determining a course of action that will successfully incorporate the knowledge from both worldviews.

Red Brother, White Brother is an invitation to explore the next step, to address the often asked question "where do we go from here?" This questions is best answered, as is fitting, by those personally affected by the system. The voices of those who have experienced the child welfare system first hand, those who have survived it, and those who have researched concrete, practical ways to improve it. Further to this, the book will delve into the "whys" of it all. Why is change not occurring? It is not from a lack of trying, nor from a lack of knowledge into what could be done differently. It is because of the attitudes and systems which remain solidly in place, preventing any meaningful change. These systems, from the iron cage of bureaucracy to systemic racism will be explored in an attempt to shed a better light on the "whys" behind the issues. This conversation would not be complete without a discussion on the drivers of change, as well as the determinants of how positive change is evaluated. Both topics are covered in these pages as well.

Finally, and perhaps most importantly, *Red Brother, White Brother* provides a myriad of realistic, concrete suggestions for meaningful changes to policy and practice in Aboriginal child welfare. The contents of these pages are partially derived from my own experiences, including over 48 years of working at all levels of child welfare, from front line worker to assistant deputy minister, from Children's Advocate to Social Work Professor. For the past 15 years I have been immersed in trying to understand the reality of the children, families and communities that are served by child welfare systems.

Through the best possible teachers, those who have survived the child welfare system, I have learned of the consequences of the mistakes made by the child welfare system. More specifically, I have learned from adult survivors of the system, a group of people who were children on my own caseload when I was a fledgling caseworker during the mid-sixties. This knowledge is as humbling as it is important. It is now my responsibility to bring to this dialogue the insights offered to me by child welfare survivors, buttressed by my own years of experience.

I gratefully and humbly thank those who shared their ideas, their experiences and their passion for change; without their contribution, this would just be another book about what "we" think "they" should do, and there is no place for any more books like that.

For those who are reading this right now, welcome to the journey, whether you are an Aboriginal person, a non-Aboriginal person, a social worker, a policy maker, a politician, or a concerned and curious member of society in general.

Red Brother, White Brother is about restoring a very severed and damaged relationship, about recognizing the impediments that remain in the way, and about finally coming together to make lives better for Aboriginal children, their families and communities.

Are you ready?

The Tale of Two Rivers

Close to the city of Manaus, Brazil, the Rio Solimoes and the Rio Negro converge to form the Amazon River. The pale, murky color of the Rio Solimoes heralds its burden of glacial silt and sand, which results from its origin in the Peruvian Andes Mountains. The dark color of the Rio Negro is characteristic of clear waters that originate in areas of basement rock and carry little sediment. East of Manaus, the pale and dark waters flow side-by-side as distinct flows before they eventually converge; even after they converge, each retains its essential quality and characteristics. The resulting foam is unique; it would not exist if the two rivers had not merged together.

My hope is that, similarly, the new knowledge generated by our coming together will allow Aboriginal and non-Aboriginal people to retain their essential qualities, while creating new solutions that will better serve all children and families.

Chapter 1

A Brief History

Key Points

1. How the residential school experience set the stage for problems today.
2. How the 60s scoop was set up to pick up the pieces.
3. How we continue to extend both systems today in spite of our best efforts.

> *"If men could learn from history, what lessons it might teach us! But passion and party blind our eyes, and the light which experience gives us is a lantern on the stern which shines only on the waves behind."*
>
> **Samuel Taylor Coleridge**

There is considerable evidence that early European arrivals formed mutually beneficial long-term alliances with native people for the purposes of trade and war. By the late 1800s, however, these alliances were no longer considered useful and the thirst for land by settlers overcame their need for alliances with Aboriginal people. It was then that new mechanisms of domination and colonization were implemented in the form of residential schools that lasted for most of the next century.

It is to this system that the notion of historic trauma is attributed. Aboriginal children were removed from their families at a young age to be raised by a system that often abused them physically, emotionally, spiritually and sexually. The primary message was that they were worthless, their parents were worthless and their culture was to be destroyed. When the residential school system was in the throes of it death rattle, it was replaced with public child welfare systems that failed to understand the extent to which Aboriginal families and communities had been decimated by the residential school experience, setting the stage for another disastrous effort to "protect" Aboriginal children.

It is important to understand what transpired in both of these events and to think of new ways to counter their negative impacts. One place to begin is by acknowledging the racist attitudes and beliefs that created the systems they engendered. Duncan Campbell Scott, Deputy Superintendent General of Indian Affairs, encapsulates the prevailing attitude of his day in 1920, during a House of Commons discussion on proposed changes to the Indian Act.

> *"Our objective is to continue until there is not a single Indian in Canada that has not been absorbed into the body politic, and there is no Indian question, and no Indian department. That is the whole object of this bill"* (Aboriginal Justice Implementation Commission, p. 6).

According to Scott and government policy, it was imperative to "kill the Indian" in the child in order to save the man and many shared the view that the young were the only hope for substantial change, as the adults were considered irredeemable and a hindrance to the civilizing process. One of the few dissenting voices among the dominant culture of the era was that of Frank Oliver, Superintendent General of Indian Affairs, who demurred in 1908, after the foundations of the residential school system had been laid in place that;

> *I hope you will excuse me for so speaking but some of the most important commandments laid upon the human by the divine are love and respect by children for parents. It seems strange that in the name of religion, a system of education should have been instituted, the foundation principle of which, not only ignored but contradicted this command.*

In spite of this caution, the residential school system was implemented. It failed to meet the prevailing standards of the day in almost every respect, and contravened standards of care in ways that that fell short the most basic humanitarian expectations including those of the Declaration of Human Rights in 1948. The creation of a "total institution" to destroy a people was a deliberate and planned effort by its architects, delivered with little regard for a people who were nearly decimated in the process and who are still to this day trying to rebuild their societies and their very lives.

This era was characterized by a tendency that continues to this day; inadequate funding on the part of the Canadian government, a lack of accountability for the quality of services, and a tendency to turn over responsibility for the delivery of services to other entities, including religious organizations, provincial governments and, currently, Indian Bands, all the while disclaiming any responsibility for the critical link between fiscal needs and program standards. The federal government has always controlled the purse strings for services to Aboriginal people, and has consistently arranged for other entities to provide these services, all the while imposing funding limitations that constrained them in ways that were fundamentally harmful to Aboriginal communities.

This cycle began when the residential schools were established; in the early 1900s, the government soon realized that they were pursuing the wrong path by re-creating a model of serving children that had already been recognized by child care professionals as damaging to children. This, however, did not deter Canada from expanding this model of child care in spite of the evidence that the children were not well served and were ill-prepared for life in contemporary society as well as in their communities of origin. It was not until the early 1940s that Canada began to press provincial authorities to assume responsibility and provide alternate care for Aboriginal children in need of protection. It took until the early 1960s for provinces to assume this role, on the condition that the federal government would reimburse them for such care. Tragically, neither level of government ensured that essential community and familial supports were available to keep families together. This led the so-called 60s Scoop, and the removal of thousands of Aboriginal children from their homes and into non-Aboriginal institutions and foster homes.

The pattern continues today, in spite of delegated authority to First Nation's communities for child welfare services, since that authority is accompanied by federal government funds intended mainly for the removal and alternate care of Aboriginal children. The failure to provide for prevention and early intervention programs that would help to keep families together continues. In addition, Aboriginal communities have been unable to form the voluntary and non-profit organizations that most other communities depend upon to support families and children. The ultimate outcome for Aboriginal children and families is the ongoing, ever increasing numbers of children lost to their communities.

In light of these historical and current events, a fundamental policy and attitudinal shift is necessary. The policy was very clear in the late 1800s; and although it has been formally changed in provincial legislation as these authorities acknowledge, to an extent, Aboriginal aspirations for autonomy and self-determination, provincial child welfare authorities, for the most part, continue to see themselves as responsible in law for the protection of all children to a greater or lesser degree. This often creates a situation whereby delegated First Nations authorities are hampered in their efforts by overly stringent and irrelevant standards of practice that do not reflect their reality or their worldview. In addition, many racist assumptions and beliefs about Aboriginal people, the very same assumptions and beliefs that created the initial child care systems, continue to be entrenched in society as a whole, permeating into the child welfare system as well.

In other words, while new policy has been formally promulgated in all provincial legislations, it has yet to permeate our hearts. While each province struggles with these issues, the federal government continues to fund programs inadequately, turning a blind eye to these policy issues as beyond its "jurisdiction", therefore foregoing its fiduciary responsibility. Local leadership at the Band level tries to deal with the immense social and economic problems, but they have little choice but to do so in a context that seems aligned against the basic interests of the community, further worsening the situation.

It is important to note that when the federal government decided to assume responsibility for Aboriginal families, they failed to understand that child rearing by several persons was a traditional custom honored and practiced by all North American Indian tribes. During periods of hunting and gathering, most nomadic tribes naturally assumed this standard of protecting children. Children were continually under the watchful eyes of tribal Elders, siblings, cousins, aunts, or grandparents. As a result of this nurturing and security, the Aboriginal child's self-concept was strongly tied to his family, clan, and tribe. Further, the extended family provided support for parents because the responsibility for raising children was shared by members of the community, and thus no single person was overloaded with the care of the children.

Parenting skills and child-rearing patterns are terms that are reflected differently in each culture. The term parenting is problematic for Aboriginal cultures. For Euro-Canadians a parent is generally a father or a mother, and the parenting role includes child-rearing; in Aboriginal cultures several members of the extended family and the community are involved in child-rearing, in spheres of activity that are considered parental in Euro-Canadian society. The broader term "child rearing" is thus a more accurate term to describe what Euro-Canadian culture considers "parenting".

Thus, the removal of Aboriginal children from parents to be raised in residential schools deprived those children of a cultural legacy. These children missed the experience of a tightly knit community of extended family and relatives who share the task of child rearing by providing nurturing and security. This deliberate assault on Aboriginal culture, tradition, language

and spirituality resulted in following outcomes for Aboriginal
people:

> *Low self-esteem; dysfunctional families and
> interpersonal relationships; parenting issues such
> as emotional coldness and rigidity; widespread
> depression; widespread rage and anger; chronic
> physical illness related to spiritual and emotional
> states; unresolved grief and loss; fear of personal
> growth, transformation and healing; unconscious
> internalization of residential school behaviors
> such as false politeness, not speaking out, passive
> compliance; patterns of paternalistic authority
> linked to passive dependency; patterns of misuse
> of power to control others, and community social
> patterns that foster whispering in the dark, but
> refusing to support and stand with those who speak
> out or challenge the status quo; the breakdown of
> the social glue that holds families and communities
> together, such as trust, common ground, shared
> purpose and direction, a vibrant ceremonial and
> civic life, co-operative networks and associations
> working for the common good, etc.; disunity and
> conflict between individuals, families and factions
> within the community; spiritual confusion; involving
> alienation from one's own spiritual life and growth
> process, as well as conflicts and confusion over
> religion; internalized sense of inferiority or aversion
> in relation to whites and especially whites in power;
> toxic communication—backbiting, gossip, criticism,
> put downs, personal attacks, sarcasm, secrets, etc.;
> becoming oppressors and abusers of others as a
> result of what was done to one in residential schools;*

> *cultural identity issues—the loss of language*
> *and cultural foundations has led to denial (by*
> *some) of the validity of one's own cultural identity*
> *(assimilation), a resulting cultural confusion and*
> *dislocation; destruction of social support networks*
> *(the cultural safety net) that individuals and*
> *families in trouble could rely upon; disconnection*
> *from the natural world (i.e. the sea, the forest, the*
> *earth, living things) as an important dimension of*
> *daily life and hence spiritual dislocation; acceptance*
> *of powerlessness within community life (Aboriginal*
> *Healing Foundation,1999).*

The abuse and neglect suffered in residential schools not only affected their lives as adults, but those of their descendants whose families have been characterized by further abuse and neglect. According to the Aboriginal Healing Foundation:

> *Intergenerational or multi-generational trauma*
> *happens when the effects of trauma are not resolved*
> *in one generation. When trauma is ignored and*
> *there is no support for dealing with it, the trauma*
> *will be passed from one generation to the next. What*
> *we learn to see as "normal" when we are children,*
> *we pass on to our own children. Children who learn*
> *that . . . or [sic] sexual abuse is "normal", and who*
> *have never dealt with the feelings that come from*
> *this, may inflict physical and sexual abuse on their*
> *own children. The unhealthy ways of behaving that*
> *people use to protect themselves can be passed on to*
> *children, without them even knowing they are doing*
> *so. This is the legacy of physical and sexual abuse in*

residential schools (Aboriginal Healing Foundation, 1999:A5).

Despite the publicity generated by the Royal Commission on Aboriginal People and the creation of the Aboriginal Healing Foundation, many non-Aboriginal people still do not understand what happened in the residential schools or how unresolved trauma from residential school abuse continues to impact individuals, families, communities and nations. It is equally important to understand that this trauma will continue to negatively impact Aboriginal communities until it can be expressed, validated and released in healthy, creative ways.

Not only would a better understanding of the historical and current impacts of this experience improve our knowledge of the past and its implications for the present, it may also provide pause for reflection on how we are be repeating past patterns because we do not yet truly understand how deeply held beliefs and assumptions may influence current practice and perpetuate similar outcomes for Aboriginal children and families today. For those who believe otherwise, consider this sobering statistic; currently, Aboriginal children enter government care in much higher numbers than at the time of the 60s Scoop.

REFLECTIONS

1. To what extent are we continuing the legacy of the residential school system?
2. What forces are contributing to this possibility?
3. What can we do to change direction and to address the forces that contribute to this possibility?

SOURCES

Aboriginal Healing Foundation. Accessible from *http://www. ahf.ca/publications/research-series*

Lafrance, J., Bastien, B., Bodor, R., & Ayala, J. (2006). Leadership Development Forums in Alberta: Making our Hearts Available from http://www.cecw-cepb.ca/sites/default/ files/publications/en/MOHS2006.pdf

Royal Commission Report on Aboriginal Peoples Available from ttp://www.ainc-inac.gc.ca/ap/rrc-eng.asp

Chapter 2

Seeing the Elephant

Key points

1. How do we "see" the entire elephant?
2. Competing drivers of change.
3. Balancing program, system, service and consumer driven change.

KNOWLEDGE MOBILIZATION

Knowledge mobilization has been actively explored in the Health field since the early 90s, but has only recently begun to attract increased attention in the field of child welfare practice. One of the challenges inherent with the field of child welfare is the complexity of issues which span multiple societal, structural, community, and emotional, mental and physical problems. Ackoff (1999) refers to child welfare as a "mess," a complex system of strongly interacting problems. To deal effectively with this "mess" the range of problems must be looked at from as many perspectives as possible.

I turn to the Hindu parable of the blind men and the elephant to illustrate further. A group of blind men stand around an elephant. Each man is tasked to touch the part of the elephant they stand before, feeling with his hands to get a sense of what that part of the elephant 'looks' like; while each blind man may get a good sense of the part of the creature they are touching, none are able to "see" what the others see. As a result, none of the men gain a clear image of the entire elephant, preventing any of them from having an understanding of what the creature is as a whole.

When considering the child welfare system, the elephant represents the system while the blind men personify the different agents of change: policy, program, service, and consumer. Each lacks a shared image of the ideal child welfare system (the elephant). Perhaps none exists. But it is suggested that an enhanced approach to Knowledge Mobilization (KM) within and between these agents of change can contribute to greater sharing of what we know about our piece of the elephant (system) while challenging our assumptions and beliefs as well as the potential shortcomings of our worldviews. Only then can we aspire to "see" the system from all perspectives and gain a better picture of what is needed.

Much of the discussion on the exchange of knowledge has focused upon the coming together of researchers and decision-makers in mutual learning in a manner that leads to improved decision-making. This proposal adds another dimension to KM; it recognizes that many others have something to contribute to the knowledge. These include, but are not limited to legislators, policy makers, program planners, program administrators, professional helpers, community members, advocates for social change, and children and families who are and/or have been served by the children's services system.

This work does not claim to have all of the answers, nor does it suggest that this is the first time that these questions have been proposed. It is but one step in the creation of greater understanding as we contemplate the next stage in the process of reconciliation and healing. There has been considerable progress, but we suggest that we still have a considerable distance to travel in our journey together.

Most people intuitively agree on important considerations in our search of better ways to serve and assist our fellow humans. This knowledge is discussed in terms of social determinants of health, attachment theory, childhood resiliency, the impact of poverty, racism and the accompanying oppression. Few can deny that our failure to address these issues can hamper the development of healthy families, which then hampers the development of healthy and productive members of our society. Yet we still seem to be stuck.

A former colleague, a crusty retired naval officer with great administrative abilities expressed it well when he said, "turning around this damn child welfare system in harder than trying to turn the Queen Mary around—in the middle of the Suez Canal!"

There are no easy answers to this conundrum, but I do wish to pose some provocative questions that will hopefully encourage us to open our minds to new *possibilities*. To follow my colleague's metaphor, two options come to mind. The first is to sail out of the canal into open water where we have the room to test ourselves with new challenges and find new places that will welcome our creativity and common sense, the path that I suspect many of our ancestors sought in coming to a new country. The second is to get out of the unwieldy Queen Mary and trade it in for a fleet of smaller craft that are more maneuverable. Perhaps in this way we can better act on what we know to be true.

COMPETING DRIVERS OF CHANGE

Up to this point, change efforts in the child welfare system have been diminished in effectiveness by the tendency to operate in isolation from other change drivers. The result of this is hampering the development of a common view and an improved understanding of the "elephant" (system). Cohen (2004) suggests that proposed strategies for reforming child welfare over the past 30 years have included new legislation, new policies and programs, more research, more resources, more litigation, and redesigning the child welfare workplace. The most striking thing about the proposed strategies was that each was presented as a self-contained solution with little recognition of the other strategies, or acknowledgement of the potential ways in which each, by itself, might fail to actually bring about reform. The various presenters appeared to be operating from very different "world views" with respect to how complex social systems work in the first place. Each perspective has its own core assumptions, its own approach to knowledge building, and its own flaws or weaknesses. Just as in the Hindu parable of the blind men and the elephant, each "sees" only a particular part of the picture, but no one sees the whole. Due to the magnitude and complexity of child welfare, it is critical that we find better ways to bring together the various perspectives into a more unified and systemic approach to change.

> *Ineffective approaches to change are self-contained solutions to a portion of the problem while ignoring the whole. These approaches fail to actually bring about reform.*

APPROACHES TO CHANGE

This section identifies four traditions of social planning and social change and relates them to different approaches to changing child welfare. John Friedmann (1987), in a sweeping account of planned change efforts, developed a framework that classifies change. According to this framework, knowledge can be derived in one of two ways, and action can take two different forms. Friedmann proposes a classification of major traditions of change via the combination of these two dimensions, knowledge and action.

1. PROGRAM DRIVEN CHANGE

Policy Analysis is an approach to planned change derived from the traditions of policy science, management science and public administration. Its adherents believe that models of social problems or situations can be constructed, and scientific analysis of data can lead to "best" solutions. Policy analysis is based on a rational problem solving approach, addressed to those in positions of power and authority. However, unlike the social reform tradition, its proposed solutions are more instrumental or program-focused and less concerned with restructuring or macro-social objectives.

The primary vehicle for change is through identifying and promoting the best policies or programs. In the child welfare field, this tradition is illustrated by those who seek to identify and evaluate programs that "work" in specific locations, then be replicated throughout the whole system. Examples of this abound in Alberta, reflecting North American and British approaches that include such models as Alberta's Family Enhancement model and Differential Response approach.

2. SYSTEMICALLY DRIVEN CHANGE

Systemically driven change promotes "grand reforms" at the macro-levels of society and assumes that that change comes from the top, therefore addressing interventions to those at high levels of power. In the case of child welfare reform, it favors large scale changes in macro-governmental policies, usually accompanied by massive infusions of new resources. It is often driven by real or perceived deficiencies in child welfare programs, usually as a result of negative publicity that creates a public lack of confidence. For example, Kamerman and Kahn (1989), following a reconnaissance of child welfare services throughout the United States, suggested that the crises in child welfare were caused by "federal policies and developments in society." In response to these findings, they called for the reformulation of social policies, including a larger role for government, requirements for stronger professional child protective services, more public funding, and more cross-system cooperation.

The primary vehicle for reform that is advocated by adherents to the Social Reform tradition is major new legislation that will mandate specific policies and structures, promote new program initiatives, or reallocate economic resources (Cohen, 2004).

Alberta can reflect upon a number of initiatives that created the momentum for such activity, such as the Richard Cardinal case that occupied media and public interest in the early 80s and ultimately paved the way for a revamped child welfare act that included a mechanism for the delegation of child welfare authority to First Nations communities.

3. SERVICE DRIVEN CHANGE

Service driven reform is derived from the American pragmatism of John Dewey's epistemology, which emphasizes that knowledge and learning are derived from "doing" or action (Dewey, 1980). Change is viewed incrementally, although from a more developmental perspective. Unlike program development, change is seen as emerging from the field rather than coming down through those in positions of central authority. Knowledge is believed to be "derived from experience and validated in practice, and therefore it is integrally a part of action" (Friedmann, 1987).

The vehicles for change in this tradition are the organizations and multi-organizational systems that are engaged in the world of practice. Alberta has much experience with this tradition as it seeks to redesign or transform how services are organized and delivered and how participation is managed among multiple stakeholders. One example is the effort to design community based partnerships that emphasize a sharing of power and responsibility for child welfare. Another is the movement to rethink the roles of the public and private sectors in the delivery of services, including the role of the private for-profit sector, through locally initiated pilot projects and continuous learning. An essential aspect of Service Driven Reform is that these efforts evolve through local experimentation rather than top-down mandates and blueprints.

4. CONSUMER DRIVEN CHANGE

Consumer driven reform begins with those who are oppressed, the marginalized members of society. While fundamental and structural changes are sought, the proposed changes are based on the knowledge and experiences of those at the bottom, rather than the authority of the state. Reform is sought through confrontation and struggle with those in positions of power; it encompasses a process of self-liberation of people in their own communities.

While the strategies of the Social Mobilization tradition often include grass roots citizen movements and nonviolent protest, in the child welfare field, the primary vehicle for organized confrontation in the U.S. in the recent past has been the class-action lawsuit that draws on the experiences of those who have been wronged or oppressed by the current system or power structure. As described by Marcia Lowry (1986), child welfare impact litigation seeks to "alter directions, and change policies, and may indeed even alter practices through *sustained and enforceable pressure*." In a case study of class action litigation against the Illinois Department of Children and Family Services, Mezey (2000) states that "child welfare litigation involves a long-term campaign for systemic reform by a politically powerless group" (p. 7). Attempts to reform child welfare systems through confrontation in the courts are one of the most prevalent reforms in the U.S. strategies today. It has been reported that during the 1990s, more than twenty-five state child welfare systems were either being sued or under federal court order due to abusive or unconstitutional practices (National Center for Youth Law, 1993). Canada, while less litigious and America, is experiencing a similar trend.

Summary of Approaches to Change

Program Driven Change	• Top down decision making • Rational problem solving approach • Focus on program and locations
Systemically Driven Change	• Top down decision making • Focus is systemic • Changes to legislation, policies and funding
Service Driven Change *	• Emerges from the field • Focus is on organizations engaged in practice
Consumer Driven Change *	• Emerges from those affected by the system • Focus on Grassroots movements, non-violent protests, class action lawsuits

* Based on the knowledge derived from the families, communities and stakeholders in the creation of this book, it is suggested that substantial change would be most successfully reached through **service and consumer driven change**.

REFLECTIONS

1. What would be the relative weight of the four change drivers on child protection today?
2. What should it be if we were to have a more balanced perspective?
3. How might we go about creating this balance?

SOURCES

Ackoff, R. (1999). *Re-Creating the Corporation.* New York: Oxford University Press.

Cohen, Burton J. (2004). Reforming the child welfare system: Competing paradigms of change. *Children and Youth Services Review. Volume 27, Issue 6,* June 2005, Pages 653-666

Friedmann, J. (1987). *Planning in the Public Domain: From Knowledge to Action.* Princeton NJ: Princeton University Press.

Mezey, S. (2000). *Pitiful Plaintiffs: Child welfare litigation and the Federal Courts.* Pittsburgh: University of Pittsburgh Press

Chapter 3

What About Relationship?

Key points

1. What was envisioned in the 80s for Aboriginal people has not yet been fully achieved.
2. It is important that we restore our severed relationship.
3. We need to implement what we know about the social determinants of health and how to ensure that our children are strong and resilient.

Quite simply stated, the state of child welfare has been one of constant crisis for much of the past two decades. This is especially true when it comes to Aboriginal children, who numbers are swelling caseloads to catastrophic levels, in spite of great efforts and investments of time, money and resources on the part of federal, provincial and local governments. There was hope in the early eighties, with the development of new enabling legislation and policy intended to create greater autonomy and self-determination for Aboriginal people, yet these changes have not come about as expected. What happened? Why have the anticipated outcomes not occurred?

There are likely many reasons, but the bottom line is that far too many Aboriginal children are entering the child welfare system. Many are placed with strangers many miles from their families and communities, only to end up on our streets and in our jails, belonging nowhere. It has even been suggested that more Aboriginal children are entering non-Aboriginal care than were ever removed to residential school, and far more than were placed during the now notorious 60s Scoop. We have to ask ourselves why this 100 year old tragedy continues, and what can be done to put a halt to this damaging cycle.

I begin the discussion with a comment from Baldwin Reichwein, a respected social worker, former director of child welfare and a leader in the planning the delegation of child welfare responsibilities to Aboriginal communities during the 1980s. Baldwin shared the following:

> *I recall the dialogue between the Aboriginal communities and governments in the 1980s, principles of the tripartite agreements, and work undertaken and recorded by and for the Working Committee on Native Child welfare and subsequent Provincial Advisory Committee on Native Issues. Having been close to the drafting and consultation of content contained in reports by both committees noted, let me quote the following concepts that were highlighted after the Richard Cardinal tragedy. "Native child welfare should be COMMUNITY-BASED AND CONTROLLED, delivered to Native families and their children within their own communities, and the nature of the services should be NATIVE DETERMINED, to be planned and developed for Native people by Native people." (IN THE INTEREST OF NATIVE CHILD WELFARE SERVICES, 1987, 14). I refer to the events because the committees had the benefit of extensive Aboriginal community consultation*

and involvement and there was an anticipation of positive changes. While undoubtedly some progress has been made since 1987, progress has fallen short of aspirations held by many Aboriginal people. Email message dated August 17, 2008.

Many of the Aboriginal Elders who were part of this movement to self-determination and autonomy are disappointed with the limited role that has been assigned to them. I recall how Mary Kappo, a respected Sturgeon Lake Elder who has become like a second mother to me, expressed this feeling of disappointment when the administration of the newly established delegated child welfare program eliminated the advisory and decision-making role of the Elders in planning for their children.

THE IMPORTANCE OF RELATIONSHIP

I wish to call your attention to a concept that, in my view, has been sadly overlooked in social policy, social work education, and social work practice for at least two decades. This is the concept of *relationship* and its fundamental relevance to all of what we do with and for each other.

The inspiration for this subject comes from the stories shared with me by those who have experienced, endured and survived the child welfare system. While each person's story, each person's journey, is unique, they all share a common denominator; they are all about relationships. They speak to the depth and meaning of these relationships; relationships made, relationships destroyed, and, perhaps, relationships restored. For the most part, however, the stories speak to the severance of what was once whole, leaving rips and jagged edges with little chance of healing.

A SEVERED RELATIONSHIP

The colonizers were able to establish residential schools, as well as all other instruments of colonization and assimilation, as a result of their ability to adhere to a dualistic worldview; this is to say that they were able to separate themselves (the subject) from those being colonized (the object). This resulted in a severed, exploitive relationship, one that shielded the colonizer from perceiving Aboriginal children and their families as being the same as themselves.

Conversely, if we were to stand in the context of a restored relationship, we could engage in a process of mutual recognition and acknowledgement. We, as subject, meet the other as subject and the objective is not to master, harness or profit from the meeting. The restored relationship involves the willingness to open ourselves to the place of another in such a way that we genuinely let the voice of another speak to us, and in such a way that we are willing to be changed when we hear that voice and experience the perspective of another.

RESTORING RELATIONSHIPS

Is it possible to restore these relationships? Sadly, in the ongoing context of providing services to Aboriginal communities and their children, it does not seem to be so. We have moved from a system of residential schools that separated children from their families, communities, beliefs, and culture to foster placements and adoptions that continued to separate children. We have moved to placing children in care in communities separate and outside of their own, further replicating the destruction and severing of that which was once whole.

So how do you begin the restoration of these relationships? While each community has to determine its own needs in turning this around, the rebuilding of cultural traditions is key, meaning that decision makers, policy makers and child welfare agencies must recognize and support this important step. The process of rebuilding will require that resources be made available directly to Aboriginal communities so that they can develop language, cultural, spiritual and educational programs. The Aboriginal Healing Foundation has taken a step in this direction, one that could benefit from community partnerships with university researchers and service providers who are sensitive to the Aboriginal reality of today.

It is also clear that Aboriginal agencies continue to operate with less adequate financial resources than non-Aboriginal agencies. The current funding formula not only restricts such agencies from offering preventive programs, it limits the flexibility necessary to offer innovative programs that are consistent with traditional values and approaches. Caught between limited federal funding and rigid provincial policies, Aboriginal communities are wedged in, unable to change course and follow their rich tradition of helping and sustaining each other. Federal and provincial authorities must be convinced of the potential efficacy of such approaches over the long term.

Further, it seems clear that many Aboriginal agencies are operating in a policy vacuum. They have not had the opportunity to develop policies, standards and protocols that are responsive to their unique situations. A collaborative effort in concert with each other would have a greater likelihood of success than isolated efforts to promote change.

In the longer term, and as an overriding principle, those involved in the system at all levels must acknowledge the significance of relationships within the scope of child welfare; our interdependence with clients, communities and stakeholders cannot be underestimated. It will be clear to anyone with even a nodding acquaintance with child welfare practice today that the importance of relationships is not reflected in the reality of practice today. In fact, relationship building is the antithesis of much of current practice. This makes it even more important from a transfer of learning perspective, since we have hesitantly dipped our toes into the unknown of community over the past decades, while remaining reluctant to experience the full immersion that is required. As a result, the core functions of child welfare have changed very little over the past century.

HOW DO YOU MEASURE RELATIONSHIP?

Over the years, many different forms of knowledge have been derived from science, from experience, and from divine revelation. Much of this knowledge has been of immense benefit to humankind, yet other forms of knowledge continue to elude us, making them difficult to analyze and apply. Upon closer examination, it appears that knowledge that is measurable, tangible and is deemed to be highly reliable and valid. Other forms of knowing, those that are subjective, qualitative in nature and difficult to measure are often relegated to a status of less importance and less usefulness overall.

This is another reason why relationships are not prioritized in child welfare organizations; the outcomes of relationships cannot be measured. Government institutions, large organizations and funding bodies require measurable outcomes to determine if their legislations, policies and programs are effective. Unfortunately, the limited scope of these audits or assessments neglects to address the most crucial aspect of effective child welfare practice, that of relationships.

One may argue that not only is it unnecessary to assess these intangible outcomes, but is irrelevant as well. Why, then, in spite of massive investments of resources, few are satisfied with the outcomes achieved by child welfare services?

Hardly a day goes by without a major child welfare crisis somewhere in the Western world. There are calls for procedural solutions or resources to minimize the repetition of 'errors' that call attention to 'deficiencies'. Child welfare audits and reviews leave a legacy of increased paperwork, to the point where the time spent on casework with clients is now far less than the time needed to document their interventions. New procedures, safeguards, protocols, training and information requirements abound. New tools are introduced; risk assessment, sophisticated information systems, rigid timelines, greater specification of responsibilities and reporting requirements, and new legislation, to name only a few. Rarely, if ever, do the recommendations focus on the quality of supportive relationships between the social workers, children and their families, caregivers, and the community.

I propose that the de-emphasis on the critical importance of relationship, between client and workers, as well as between families, has a detrimental effect on program quality and accountability. This proposal is based on the belief that most of the problems encountered in child welfare practice are problems grounded in the quality of relationships; between parents and children, between families and communities, between communities and society, and between professionals and those they assist. The evaluation of relationship will be further explored in chapter 11, in a discussion on horizontal systems.

Rarely, if ever, do recommendations for change focus on the quality of supportive relationships between the social workers, children and their families, caregivers, and the community.

We will now focus on important considerations in our search of better ways to serve and assist our fellow humans. We will discuss such knowledge as the social determinants of health, attachment theory, childhood resiliency, the impact of poverty, racism and its accompanying oppression. Few of us can deny that these are important factors whose absence can hamper the development of healthy families, families that may otherwise be capable of forming and nurturing healthy and productive members of our society. Indeed, I would suggest that these are fundamental to lasting change in our service system for children and their families.

PREREQUISITES FOR CHANGE: THE SOCIAL DETERMINANTS OF HEALTH

Studies on the social determinants of health indicate that poverty is a major contributor to many difficulties that families experience. There is little doubt that children who are born in poor families, whose lives begin in an environment of deficiency and whose parents are preoccupied with the stresses of being able to provide decent accommodation, food, and security are at far greater risk than children whose parents are financially secure. Yet we have failed as a society to ensure that every child receives a basic level of sustenance, often blaming their parents for their deficiencies, not taking into consideration that the parents were raised within a similar situation. This is not to suggest that all poor children are doomed to the same eventuality, as some can overcome this burden at great personal effort, but we do know that there is a much higher possibility of a negative outcome.

We know that children who do not develop a sound attachment and secure base at an emotional level with their mother, especially in the womb and during the first year of life, are at an immense disadvantage, one that can be difficult to recoup. Yet we too often fail to ensure that pregnant mothers are provided with the security they need to prepare themselves for the most important job in the world, that of producing and raising the next generation of human beings. We know that children have certain developmental stages in early life during which time their brain has windows of opportunity in which to develop; when those windows of opportunity are missed, they cannot easily be recovered.

We know from resiliency theory that a child who has one person in their life who values them, respects them, and hears them makes a significant difference in that child's life. It increases the likelihood that the child will become a strong, capable individual, better prepared to face life on life's terms. Is it so difficult to ensure that every child has a special connection with one person? What about the other connections that a child needs to thrive, rather than simply survive? We know that children who have an opportunity to contribute to their community in some way have more respect for that community. They become more attached to the community, more loyal to it and will want to continue contributing with a greater sense of self-respect and belonging. We know that children who have some form of spiritual or religious connection do far better in life; with something to believe in, hope becomes more possible than otherwise. We know that children who have the opportunity to develop one talent, to have one thing they can say "I'm good at [soccer, guitar, dancing], and I like doing this" have better self-esteem. Anything that gives the child a sense of competence will help prepare the child for life on life's terms. Children who have an opportunity to engage in organized recreation are far better prepared to live life on life's terms. The evidence is incontrovertible; the lessons learned in teamwork and socialization; respect for others, competition, and channeled aggression are invaluable life lessons, lessons that every child is deserving of learning.

Yet in spite of knowing that the social circumstances of children can determine their present and future health, knowing that the happiness, contentment, and security of the mother has a huge effect on determining the future emotional and physical well-being of the child, knowing that we have limited time and opportunity to ensure that young children are able to develop to the fullest extent, we continue to fail many of our children.

Nowhere is this more visible than in the world of child welfare which deals with children who are most likely to have experienced such losses; children who are most likely to have lacked the fundamental security and firm foundations that all of us depend upon to live rich and fruitful lives. Nowhere is this more likely to happen than with children whose basic needs for security, love, food, attention, and attachment have not been met. Nowhere is this more likely to occur than with children who live with a series of unrelated caregivers, whose love and emotional attachment may be peripheral at best. Nowhere is this more likely to occur than for Aboriginal children who, in addition to the burden that they carry as a result of their early backgrounds, have to carry the burden of losing their identity, their sense of self, and their connection to family, community, and culture. The evidence seems clear that for too many of these children, life becomes a revolving door of renewed poverty, homelessness, addiction, institutional life in jails and mental health settings. This we know to be true.

We have come to realize that much of the neglect experienced by Aboriginal children is related to the intergenerational transmission of trauma in their families and communities; to the poverty of their families that results in poor housing in risk-filled neighborhoods, inadequate nutrition, and social marginalization; to social isolation, to the generations of Aboriginal mothers have given birth in an environment of so much violence and fear that they seek a false sense of safety in the bottle or the needle; to the inherent racism that we do not speak of, but that must be confronted if we are ever to progress as a nation.

It would be wonderful to say that we are addressing these issues in anything but a patchwork basis. But we are not. Our present child protection system is focused on a limited mandate restricted to the protection of children who are at risk; this mandate does not, however, take these larger issues into consideration. When the child protection system and the families it serves are overwhelmed by seemingly intractable social problems, the tendency to restrict the level and scope of intervention can seem rational and unavoidable. Yet this does not resolve these problems, does it?

Instead, this increasingly forensic approach to the delivery of child protection service (CPS) tends to focus on the parent as villain and on the gathering of evidence to confirm their deficiencies to the point where court action and the heavy hand of the law become the preferred option. When asked about what interventions are most utilized in CPS, the responses of practitioners are not encouraging. Endless rounds of parenting classes, anger management, alcohol and drug rehabilitation, drug testing, and in-home support services are implemented. Too often the 'casework' process involves nothing more than the imposition of such services rather than a problem solving process with the parents, the extended family and the community. Without a collaborative problem solving approach, how can we find innovative ways to address the real problems?

Across this continent and beyond, the following themes in the literature regarding the concerning trend of caseload growth were repeated with notable frequency. In no particular order, they are:

- Poverty is a universal variable,
- Poverty is the most important contributor to child neglect,
- All children living in poverty are not at risk, but children who are part of the child protection world are overwhelmingly from poor families,
- Child welfare referrals invariably increase in times of economic distress, when eligibility for assistance is narrowed, and/or public assistance rates are decreased,
- Little progress will be made in protecting our children until we are able to ensure that their parents are in a position to provide for their basic needs.

Julia Lathrop said it just as clearly in 1919 as head of the newly formed Children's Bureau in the U.S.: "Children are not safe and happy if their parents are miserable, and parents must be miserable if they cannot protect a home against poverty. Let us not deceive ourselves: the power to maintain a decent family living standard is a primary essential of child welfare."

Some have defined wisdom as the ability to apply knowledge into practice. My question is, when does this knowledge turn into wisdom? We know that Indigenous people everywhere are suffering. We know that twenty percent of the world population are consuming eighty percent of the world's resources. We know that we are devastating Mother Earth in our practices, fouling her waters, polluting her air. We know that there are fundamental racist and oppressive attitudes towards others, particularly towards those with a darker shade of skin. We know that many of our mainstream institutions function based on the constant supply of such people to maintain their existence. Our courts, our legal systems, our police forces, our jails depend upon a constant and increasing supply to keep their jobs. We also know that the solutions do not lie in the arrest, processing, and incarceration of poor black, Native, and Hispanic men. Nor do the solutions lie in continuing to remove Aboriginal children from their families and communities. The evidence seems clear that the solutions sought by the Bush administration, and now the Harper administration, the expenditure of billions in treasure to build more jails that will house the products of our residential schools and child welfare systems will not address the problems and the issues that are ahead of us.

REFLECTIONS

1. Is it so difficult to ensure that children can contribute something to their community, to their school, to their church . . . to themselves?
2. Is it so difficult to ensure that every child has the opportunity to live life fully?
3. Why do we have so much trouble changing our minds in the face of so much evidence that what we do now is not working?

SOURCES

Coulton, Claudia et al. 1995. "Community level factors and child maltreatment rates." *Child Development* 66(5): 1262-1276

Drake, Brett and Pandey, Shanta. 1996. "Understanding the relationship between neighborhood poverty and specific types of child maltreatment." *Child Abuse and Neglect* 20(11): 1003-1018;

Goldman, Salus and Wolcott Kennedy. 2003. *A Coordinated Response to Child Abuse and Neglect: The Foundation for Practice.* Office on Child Abuse and Neglect (DHHS)

Novick, Marvyn and Shillington, Richard. 1996. *Crossroads for Canada: A Time to Invest in Children and Families.* Toronto: Campaign 2000.

PART II

The experience of
Aboriginal People with
Child Welfare

The fundamental premise in reviewing the following is to illustrate that the helping process is influenced by three factors: the methodology or technique applied, the relationships involved, and the context in which the work takes place. Of these factors, the context accounts for 45% of the process, the relationships involve 40% and the techniques count for a mere 15%.

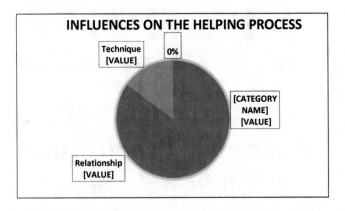

The key message of those who work with or experience our interventions is very congruent with this belief. The work and social context in which these interactions take place have a tremendous impact. This ranges from the office settings and environment of professional staff as well as the community settings of the families served. Similarly, the relationships between social workers themselves and their leaders, as well as with the families and communities they serve, are of critical importance. Equally important are the relationships of people with others in their communities, where day to day discourse takes place.

Least important are the various methodologies, techniques and procedures that must be followed. Yet it seems at times that these are what receive the most attention. Information systems, 'new' casework and assessment models, revised organizational and service delivery approaches take up precious time and energy, all the while discounting what is clearly of most importance in improving outcomes for Aboriginal families in the child welfare system.

The next section will describe how the child welfare system appears to the families now being served, those who have been there as children, the communities who have lost their children and those unsung heroes who labor valiantly trying to make it all work—child welfare workers.

Chapter 4

Insights from Aboriginal Mothers

Key points

1. There is considerable theoretical information that the assumptions made about Aboriginal mothers and the imposition of a world view that is foreign to them places them at a great disadvantage.
2. Research on Aboriginal mothers in B.C., Alberta and Manitoba indicates that such women are often treated with considerable disrespect.
3. It seems clear that our efforts to work with them is seen as unhelpful and often causes more harm than good.
4. These mothers have some interesting ideas to consider from a policy and program perspective that deserve to be heard.

This chapter takes us to a group that receives very little attention from decision makers and policy makers; the Aboriginal mothers of children involved with the child welfare system. This is an important voice, and it needs to be heard. After all, this is where all Aboriginal children begin their life on earth; it is also who they are removed from when they enter the child welfare system. When one considers that the decision to bring children into care is made between the child welfare worker and the mother, it should be the most important voice for policy makers and decision makers to hear.

When one reflects upon the critical importance of the encounter between a front-line child welfare worker and an Aboriginal mother, the subsequent decisions that are made are of critical importance from an emotional, social, and even fiscal perspective. Each decision can have million dollar repercussions when considered from a long term perspective, given the potential impacts down the road for the family, the children and the subsequent generations.

Aside from the more systemic considerations mentioned earlier in this document, our attitudes and responses to the mothers of Aboriginal children, who are the source of 70% of the children in the care of children's services in Alberta. The proportion in our neighboring provinces is even higher. If one assumes that children in care account for approximately 60% of the child welfare budget, we are looking at about six hundred million dollars in direct costs. When we consider all of the associated health, education, and justice costs, when we take into account that many of the children who spend their lives in permanent care, as Aboriginal children tend to do, end up in our correctional facilities, addicted, homeless, and belonging nowhere, the fiscal considerations alone boggle the mind. And this does not begin to address the social costs of losing the future contribution of these children at a time when our aging population will need every one of our youth to become healthy and contributing members of our society.

70% of Alberta's children *in care* are Aboriginal, yet only 9% of the children in Alberta are Aboriginal.

¹This chapter is draws primarily on a study conducted in Manitoba about the experience of Aboriginal mothers involved with the child welfare system. In addition I have examined the reports entitled *Broken Promises: Parents Speak about B.C.s Child welfare System (2008)* prepared by the Pivot Legal Society and the Alberta study entitled *Broken Hearts,* which has produced a film by the same name and a guide for Aboriginal mothers and their child welfare workers. The Pivot Legal Society report can be accessed at http://www.pivotlegal.org/Publications/reportsbp.htm.

The findings are similar in each province, and although we cannot generalize this information, there are sufficient commonalities in the experiences of Aboriginal mothers in three western provinces to suggest that this calls for closer examination. The triangulation of data from three different settings adds sufficient credibility to serve as a caution, not unlike a dying canary in a mine which warns the miners of toxic gases that may soon overwhelm them. These studies collectively and individually serve as a warning that much of our work with Aboriginal mothers is, to say the least, not helpful. Some would say it is, in fact, toxic.

---

¹   This information draws from an article entitled Jumping through Hoops, a Manitoba study examining the experiences and reflections of Aboriginal mothers involved with child welfare and legal systems respecting child protections matters. It is based upon a project report prepared for Ka Ni Kanichik Inc. and the Steering Committee of the Family Court Diversion Project by Marlyn Bennett of the First Nations Child & Family Caring Society dated July 8, 2008. The full text is available from **http://www.fncfcs.com/projects/FNRS.html**

There is no reason to believe that the situation is any different in all jurisdictions in the U.S., Australia, and New Zealand. Interestingly, there are parallels in all of the English speaking countries that were colonized by the British.

THEORETICAL BACKGROUND TO THE STUDIES

Many of the women who participated in the Manitoba study were survivors of childhood abuse, either physical, sexual or both. Some were still learning to deal with the ramifications of these experiences in their own lives at the time their children became involved with the child welfare system. Some of the mothers had themselves been in care as children, and many had been exposed to various forms of abuse while they were in care. It seems likely that many of the mothers have been victims of the intergenerational transmission of trauma that began in the residential schools.

Bennett (2008) draws extensively on Kline(1989, 1990, 1993) and others (Cull, 2006; Kellington, 2002; MacDonald, 2002; Monture-Angus, 2002) who challenge the existing approach to Aboriginal mothers and the assumptions about what made a "good mother", including the ideology of motherhood held by courts as being one of "motherly self-sacrifice" and assumptions that all mothers belonged to a nuclear family. Kline (1989) indicated that this ideology was an improper yardstick to use for Aboriginal mothers, particularly as the "sacrifice" or responsibility of child-rearing is viewed by Aboriginal families as being one that is shared.

Kline (1990) clearly analyzed the centrality of the 'best interests of the child' doctrine as applied in First Nations child welfare cases. The substance of Kline's thesis deduced that this doctrine is a major contributing factor in the destructive and assimilationist impacts of the child welfare system on First Nations children and families. The judicial decision-making has downplayed, if not completely negated, the relevance and importance of maintaining a child's First Nations identity and culture.

Kline (1993) argued that dominant ideologies of motherhood are imposed on First Nations women in child welfare cases. First, Kline observed that the law created a conceptual framework within which First Nations women are blamed for the difficulties they experience in child-raising, which in turn obfuscates the roots of those difficulties in the history and current dynamics of colonialism and racial oppression. Secondly, Kline pointed out that "the ideology of motherhood operates to impose dominant culture values and practices in relation to child-raising in First Nations families, and conversely to devalue different values and practices of First Nations families. The combined effect of these two processes is to leave First Nations women particularly vulnerable to being constructed by courts as 'bad mothers' in child welfare proceedings, and consequently open to having their children taken away as a result" (p. 306).

Some of the ways that mothers coped with the stress of child welfare intervention in their lives were also identified. The recommendations suggested by the mothers who participated in this study include ideas on how to implement more comprehensive and broad-ranging preventative services that would be useful and would impact on mothers and children in a more positive way than what currently exists. Current punitive approaches in child welfare do little to produce healthy, productive members of society, and punishing women is all too often what happens (Cull, 2006). Women indicated that direct services should be aimed directly at parents as a means of ensuring that resources also reach their children. Another recommendation included instituting a "Mothers' Advocate Office" to provide mothers with a stronger voice in articulating their needs and concerns at the policy-making and developmental levels of government. Their recommendations also reiterate that there need to be better resources and protection for those responsible for raising children.

In some cases, women reported that it was unclear to them as to why their children had been removed. Most of the removals were court ordered and very few mothers were given the option of voluntarily placing their children in care while they dealt with their underlying issues.

Many of the Aboriginal mothers expressed that the manner in which their children were apprehended was traumatic. Mothers' perceptions were that the child abuse investigations were inadequate and missed important information. Many mothers expressed frustration at what they perceived as the social worker's changing expectations, and what they perceived as a lack of attention to the mother's concerns. Mothers shared that they endured numerous changes with respect to the social workers assigned to their case, resulting in their children staying in care longer. This also contributed to difficulties in developing trust in the Ministry. Mothers noted that their social workers were often young, making it difficult to relate to them. Racism and disrespect toward Aboriginal mothers were also evident in many of the stories.

One participant in particular shared that the "social worker I dealt with was condescending, rude, disrespectful of me in front of my children. She attacked my parenting; she attacked everything about me in front of my children" (p. 31).

Many of the mothers talked about the emotional repercussions from losing their children. These emotional repercussions centered on grief, loss and the guilt associated with the removal of their children. Here is a summary of what the mother's expressed feeling as a result of losing their children:

- Aboriginal mothers need to have more opportunities to express and deal with the pain of losing their children through the child protection process; they also need opportunities to heal from this pain.
- Mothers feel and experience the same level of psychological ramifications from removal as do the children who are removed.
- Mothers are concerned about the placement of their children in non-Aboriginal homes.
- Mothers are frustrated at not being consulted with respect to the plans made for their children while in care.
- Those able to make arrangements to place their children with family members met with frustration due to the enormous amount of energy and effort it took to have their children placed with kin.
- Sometimes the homes in which Aboriginal children were placed were arguably more harmful to the children than their own homes.
- Many of the Aboriginal mothers involved in this study were unable to get any information about their children while in care and after children were returned.

MOTHER'S EXPERIENCES
WITH CHILD WELFARE

FEAR OF CHILD WELFARE

Mothers expressed great fears around child welfare intervention. Mothers indicated they were afraid to get help from child and family services. Mothers stated they were afraid to seek out treatment for fear that their children would be apprehended if they sought out this needed assistance. This is reflected in the following comment:

> *I was even scared to go for treatment because I figured . . . if I'm going to go for treatment then it means I got a problem and they're going to find a reason to take my kids away and that's what happened, right. I . . . tried to do that anyway and then they wound up taking my kids away so . . . so either way, I just kind of . . . had this feeling that . . . I had to stop what I was doing but I didn't know how and I didn't know where to go. I didn't know who to trust cause I was alone.*

BEING MONITORED

A few of the mothers' narratives speak of being subjected to numerous drug and alcohol testing by the child welfare agency's staff. One mother in particular stated that she was required to undergo random drug testing at least three times a month by the child welfare agency involved with her family. Closely related to drug and alcohol testing was the feeling of being watched by child welfare. Mothers felt strongly that being under scrutiny was an invasion of their privacy, as was noted by this mother:

> *. . . and they always managed to get me to that point because they knew I had company, they would get somebody to spy on my home, they knew people were coming in there, they had specific names. They had people watching my home and I'm going to try to make a court case saying that's invasion of my privacy and movement. A bunch of people that are watching my home that are watching what is going on, coming in and out of my house.*

TRIGGERING MOTHERS' ANGER

Others noted that it appeared to them that the social workers deliberately tried to make them angry. Social workers, it appeared to the mothers in this study, did everything in their power to trigger anger as this mother reflected.

> *They want to set you up. There are key words and there are key things they try to throw at you to make you fly off the handle. I'm not stupid, I know their game.*

VISITATION ARRANGEMENTS

Mothers who participated in the interviews and talking circles unanimously conceded experiencing many problems and difficulties around their visitation rights. Visits were inconsistent, held infrequently, and were often too short. Mothers stated that visits were often supervised and took place in the office of the child welfare agency they were dealing with.

> *I looked forward to the Saturday visitations I had with them for an hour. That was very hard, very hard. To see them crying because they had to leave me and it's not like I could walk to a park and be alone with them, I had to be supervised. I'm not an abusive mom . . . that I could not understand. What did they think I was going to do with my kids? It was awful.*

HARM TO CHILDREN WHILE IN CARE

In addition to the pain and loss experienced by Aboriginal mothers when their children were removed, many mothers expressed fear and concern over the impact of the removal on their children. The most frequently cited worry that mothers brought to our attention was the possibility that their children may have been or were sexually abused while in care.

> *At one point my family had to intervene because my kids were in a foster home where it was a cult. There was sexual abuse going on, there was physical abuse going on, the foster mom actually got her licensed pulled . . . a lot of my son's and my daughter's psychological abuse and physical abuse stemmed from that particular foster home.*

Mothers say the biggest impact on children as a result of being removed is the loss of the development of deeper relationships with family, as this mother lamented.

> *My 18 year old son grew up in the child welfare system. My son . . . has a lot of anger and abandonment issues . . . But he always has a safe home to come home to. I still love him and I'll always be here . . . he has trust issues. He does come home but when he does come home, all he does is he showers, packs clothes and then he leaves. I have not had a relationship with my son and I blame the child welfare system for that.*

CHILD WELFARE EXPECTATIONS AND PROGRAMMING

Many of the mothers shared with us that they attended numerous programs at the request of the child welfare worker and agency. There is a sense that there is no rhyme and reason to the types and/or number of programs that mothers are required to attend. For many of the mothers it seemed that they were over-programmed and the child welfare expectations seemed to change from month to month.

> *I had to jump through hoops . . . going through parenting programs . . . I don't even know how many programs . . . I went for treatment . . . I got so many certificates it's unreal.*

Another mother explained she was exhausted from all the programming she had to attend.

> *I've been through so many programs in the last three months. Sometimes I barely ate. I've even barely slept. I went from 8, 9 o'clock in the morning*

> *right to 9:30 at night. Sometimes all day long from*
> *3 programs a day. Then I get up and have to go to*
> *another one. But I did it! I'm glad I did it. And I told*
> *[my worker] I'm just so programmed out.*

JUMPING THROUGH HOOPS

Mothers reported feeling that they had to jump through hoops and play the game to satisfy child welfare, whether that meant taking more programming or just, it seemed, to satisfy the whim of social workers to prove they were doing what needed to be done to get their children returned or to ensure visits with children currently in care. This was a comment made so often by the mothers we interviewed that it became the central title of the final report in Manitoba and is reflected in the following comments made by some of the mothers in this study.

> *You're a person who's trying to live your life*
> *and then you're going to try and jump through*
> *hoops . . . this jumping through hoops business was*
> *getting me mad.*

> *He wanted me to jump through hoops and I didn't't*
> *like . . . You have to try and prove to them that*
> *you're trying to get them back and you're trying to*
> *do everything they want you to do. In order to do*
> *that you've got to . . . I felt like I was always kissing*
> *their ass . . .*

> *I have never, ever once had a good experience with*
> *Child and Family, never with anything. If the kids are*
> *taken it takes so much to even try to get to see them*
> *and put it this way . . . you've got to jump through*
> *hoops to even try and get a visit with your kids.*

> *It's just one frustration after another. It's like you*
> *have to jump through hoops . . . they don't tell you*
> *exactly what it is that they want . . .*

LACK OF AWARENESS REGARDING RIGHTS

Mothers stated that when their children were first apprehended by child and family services they did not know where to turn to for help and assistance. They were not sure how to obtain a lawyer or where to get Legal Aid assistance, and the child welfare social workers they came into contact with were unhelpful in providing the information mothers' needed to help themselves understand what to do next. They did not know what their rights were.

> *I didn't't know any of my rights. I didn't know I*
> *could have hired a lawyer. I could have had support*
> *services come in . . . CFS didn't sit down and say*
> *"look we can give you a support worker; we can*
> *suggest this program and that program to you."*
> *None of that was done. It was just "okay, here's a*
> *court date, come for your kids."*

Aboriginal mothers had made many comments about the quality of services provided by the Legal Aid lawyers who represented them in child protection matters before the courts. The comments about their lawyers were positive as well as negative. However, evaluation of the quality of legal services received was primarily negative. Many mothers indicated that their lawyers did not appear to represent them. Many said their lawyers counseled them to agree with the decisions made by the child welfare agency. For many, it appeared that the lawyers worked for child welfare agencies and that many of the decisions were made in consultation with the child welfare agencies rather than with the mothers they represented, as these mothers adamantly stated:

> *I don't know who told me . . . they said [the lawyer]*
> *works for Child and Family Services . . . wouldn't*
> *that be a conflict of interest for her to take my case*
> *against them because she works for them? All she*
> *was trying to do was make me sign papers to do*
> *whatever they wanted. I knew deep down inside no*
> *I'm not doing it I don't feel right about it.*

In addition to the confusing terminology used the court room, mothers indicated that they did not feel their lawyers did enough to defend or represent them in court:

> *My lawyer was just doing whatever . . . it's not fair*
> *because if the social worker's allowed to talk to*
> *them why can you not defend yourself and then*
> *have them already swaying the judge because they*
> *are so educated they know exactly what to say.*
> *Meanwhile, half of those words you don't even*
> *understand. You're supposed to be up there trying*
> *to get your lawyer to defend you and you don't even*
> *know half the words that they're saying. When I sat*

> *there the first time . . . why the hell is my lawyer*
> *not saying anything? What's going on here? It's just*
> *the one thing that the judge hears and that's it. Your*
> *lawyer's not defending you because she's working for*
> *them . . . it's a no win situation.*

In many instances, mothers indicated that they had minimal amount of time with their lawyers prior to the courtroom experiences and many felt their lawyers were essentially strangers who did not provide them with the sort of strength, comfort and friendship they needed under the circumstances.

> *I wasn't looking for sympathy, but there was never . . .*
> *not even . . . a friendship thing with my lawyer . . . it*
> *was just more business.*

The majority of mothers agreed that family law courts are not an appropriate environment to oversee child protection issues involving Aboriginal families. The court was a very intimidating experience where many felt harshly judged. Their collective perceptions center around the belief that the decisions made by judges within the court setting are racist, biased and one sided in favor of the child welfare agencies interpretation of the situation. Judgment came not only from judges and child welfare staff but also extended to their own lawyers.

LACK OF COURTROOM SUPPORTS AND ADVOCATES

Women reported not being allowed to bring supportive people with them when they went into the courtroom to face the judge, lawyers, child welfare staff and numerous other courtroom personnel and/or witnesses.

> *The advocate . . . wasn't allowed in the courtroom.*
> *Well . . . what I said was, "oh, you guys are allowed*
> *all your people but I'm not allowed to have mine?"*
> *I think it is important for these women to have*
> *someone there with them because they become*
> *emotional . . . you've got these people bashing*
> *you, your character and your parenting. You need*
> *someone there! They need to change that, definitely.*
> *You should be allowed whoever you want in court*
> *with you and maybe you're not allowed 10 people,*
> *or 5 people, but at least 2 people should be allowed,*
> *or 3 even, your lawyer and 2 other people.*

KNOWLEDGE OF ALTERNATIVE DISPUTE RESOLUTIONS

None of the mothers interviewed for this study were aware of the various alternative dispute resolutions (i.e. mediation or family group conferencing) that could be utilized in the child welfare context. Aboriginal mothers reported that child welfare staff and lawyers rarely offered and/or made suggestions to alleviate the tension that is inherent throughout the child welfare experience. The only alternative was really no alternative as this mother noted:

> *I don't know any alternatives other than going*
> *to court and trying to fight and saying no, I want*
> *my kid back and that is the only thing I know . . . I*
> *know a little bit about restorative justice because I*

> *was part of stuff like for a number of years before.*
> *But there's nothing. I don't know what there is . . .*
> *for someone in my situation. I felt like there was*
> *literally a 10 foot, 20 foot brick wall all the way*
> *around me and I couldn't't get out and that's a really*
> *horrible suffocating feeling you know, when you*
> *know there's no way out. You've got to . . . the only*
> *way is their way and . . . they're the law, they're the*
> *justice system.*

Regardless of the time children spend in care, mothers are very optimistic that they will resume a relationship with their children when they come of age. Despite their circumstances, the mothers we spoke to were optimistic; they prayed and continue to work on themselves to become strong for when that day comes, as this mother poignantly shared:

> *It hurts but I know one day my children are going*
> *to be 18. If they turn 18 and they decide to come*
> *home, I want to be mentally and physically ready*
> *for my children. And I want to be healthy for my*
> *children. So I know I have a lot of healing and work*
> *to do on myself.*

MOTHERS' RECOMMENDATIONS AND SOLUTIONS FOR CHANGE

This study gave Aboriginal mothers an opportunity to voice their perspectives about their experiences and to suggest simple changes and solutions for helping other mothers to understand the child welfare system. The following recommendations were formulated from the responses provided by the mothers during the talking circles and interviews, augmented by the researcher's observations, and analyses of the findings. There are seven recommendations in all:

1. **Development of an Aboriginal Mothers' Advocates Office/Institute:** This would involve the development of a formal organization to assist Aboriginal mothers in navigating all aspects and complexities of the child welfare system within the province of Manitoba.

2. **Establishment of a training program for the Aboriginal Mothers' Advocates:** The Aboriginal Mother's Advocates Office would, in addition to other purposes, be responsible for training Aboriginal mothers to become advocates for the proposed Aboriginal Mothers' Advocates Office. It was suggested by the mothers in this study that advocates be mothers who have intimate knowledge and experience dealing with the child welfare and legal systems.

3. **Development of a manual on understanding the child welfare and legal systems:** Development of a manual outlining what Aboriginal mother's can expect in terms of the child welfare/court processes including: 1) time lines: 2) user friendly terms and definitions; 3) information on the legal process; 4) information on how to access and instruct legal counsel; and 5) information on access to programs and treatment resources for Aboriginal mothers involved with the child welfare system.

4. **Development of mothers' support groups:** The mothers in this study identified the need to develop

more support groups across the province for Aboriginal mothers/grandmothers involved with the child welfare system. These support groups would meet monthly and act as an information and support forum for women to meet and learn from other women who've had similar experiences.

5. **Courtroom advocates:** Mothers in this study suggested that in addition to their lawyers and the Aboriginal mother's advocates, close family, friends and other supporters should be allowed into courtrooms.

6. **Development of a website:** The website would include information about the Aboriginal Mother's Advocates Office, courtroom advocates, and training opportunities. It would have a calendar of activities for the support groups and a listing of the resources, as well as programs and treatment options available to Aboriginal mothers involved with child welfare within the province of Manitoba. A listing and link to the contact information of lawyers who specialize in child welfare matters should also be included.

7. **Development of an anthology of Aboriginal mothers/grandmothers' stories and experiences:** There are very few resources that celebrate what it means to be an Aboriginal mother and grandmother. The last recommendation would see the creation of a book that focuses on providing Aboriginal mothers and grandmothers with a chance to share stories that reflect on the challenges, strengths and the resilience of Aboriginal mothers and grandmothers.

DISCUSSION

These stories are useful in understanding the practices that have been inflicted on Aboriginal mothers in other child welfare jurisdictions. Their stories can be a tool to begin the process of gaining awareness and understanding. I encourage the reader to refer to the Manitoba and BC studies as rich sources of knowledge for practitioners, administrators, policy makers and decision-makers; indeed, for all of us who have an interest in the well-being and future of Aboriginal children.

In 2002, K.A. MacDonald released a publication called *Missing Voices: Aboriginal Mothers Who Have Been at Risk of or Who Have Had Their Children Removed from Their Care.* MacDonald's elucidation of stories on child welfare experiences and questions on how to move forward helped Aboriginal women in moving beyond the pain of colonization and remembering trauma inflicted by the child welfare system. The recommendations, directed specifically at social workers by the Aboriginal mothers in MacDonald's study, include a need for the following:

- Cross cultural, sensitivity, and anti-racism training for social workers;
- Specific training for social workers on alcohol and drug addiction;
- Sensitivity training on the unique stresses of parenting and poverty;
- Training on how to empower and engage Aboriginal mothers in determining and designing their own "expectations";
- Discussion and explanations by social workers as to mother's legal rights;

- Support to ensure that grief, loss and counseling is provided to Aboriginal mothers upon removal of their children.

REFLECTIONS

The implications from a policy and program development perspective have immense ramifications. Aside from human justice issues identified in these reports and the obvious fiscal considerations that should be of interest to provincial ministries responsible for child protection programs, the following questions come to mind:

1. Why do social workers and mothers have to be adversaries in this process?
2. Why is there such a reluctance to utilize family conferencing as a treatment modality when it seems so aligned with Aboriginal culture, traditions and values?
3. Why are we waiting to have Mother's Advocates? If we could extricate ourselves from the adversarial process, why could the child welfare worker not be the mother's advocate?
4. What is stopping us from providing mothers with easily understood information about the workings of the system so they know what they are dealing with?
5. Do we know how helpful all these 'hoops' are? Recent research indicates that there are diminishing returns for having parents enrolled in too many programs, resulting in a shotgun approach that is largely ineffective.
6. How can we better teach our child welfare workers to balance their helping and authoritative roles? This has always been a cornerstone of child welfare practice.

7. How do we find more respectful ways for mothers and their children to keep in touch with each other?

SOURCES

M. Bennett, M. (2008). *Jumping Through Hoops: A Manitoba Study Examining Experiences and Reflections of Aboriginal Mothers Involved with the Child welfare and Legal Systems Respecting Child Protection Matters.* Report prepared for Ka Ni Kanichihk Inc. and the Steering Committee of the Family Court Diversion Project. Winnipeg, MB: Ka Ni Kanichihk Inc.

Broken Promises (2008). *Parents speak about B.C.'s Child welfare System.* Published February 2008 by Pivot Legal Society. http://www.pivotlegal.org/Publications/reportsbp.htm

Broken Hearts (2009). Knowing Your Rights: Child welfare Information Booklet. Published by the Creating Hope Society. www.creatinghopesociety.ca

Cull, R. (2006). Aboriginal mothering under the state's gaze. In Lavell-Harvard, D.M. and Corbiere Lavell, J. (Eds.), Until our hearts are on the ground: Aboriginal mothering, oppression, resistance and rebirth, pp. 141-156. Toronto, ON: Demeter Press.

Kellington, S. (2002). Missing Voices: Mothers at risk for or experiencing apprehension in the child welfare system in BC. Vancouver: National Action Committee on the Status of Women.

Kline, M. (1989). Child welfare law, "Best Interests of the Child" ideology, and First Nations." Osgoode Hall Law Journal, 30 (2): 375-425.

Kline, M. (1990). Child welfare law, ideology and the First Nations. Thesis (LL.M.)—York University.

Kline, M. (1993). Complicating the ideology of motherhood: Child welfare law and First Nation women. Queen's Law Journal, 18: 306-342.

MacDonald, K. A. (2002). Missing Voices: Aboriginal Mothers Who Have Been at Risk of or Who Have Had Their Children Removed from Their Care. Vancouver, BC: NAC-BC.

Monture-Angus, P. (1989). A vicious circle: Child welfare and the First Nations. Canadian Journal of Women & the Law, 3: 1-17.

Monture-Angus, P. (1995). Organizing against oppression: Aboriginal women and the Canadian state for First Nation women. In P. Monture-Angus (Ed.), Thunder in my soul: A Mohawk woman speaks. Halifax: Fernwood Publishing.

Monture-Angus, P. (1989). A vicious circle: Child welfare and the First Nations. Canadian Journal of Women & the Law, 3: 1-17.

Chapter 5

Aboriginal Community Perspectives; Making Our Hearts Sing

Key Points

1. The recovery of the Aboriginal way of life is critical to the well-being of families and communities.
2. The structural violence of colonial policies must be addressed if progress it to be made.

What is the perspective of Aboriginal communities? It would be impossible to adequately reply to this question in light of the many groups of Aboriginal people across Canada. The rich diversity of Aboriginal people cannot possibly allow any comprehensive response to this question. However, the communities of the Blood Tribe (Kainai Nation), the Sturgeon Lake Cree Nation, and the Métis Settlements have participated in community based research that has provided significant insight into their vision for the future. The following provides a brief overview of their perspective in their search for greater autonomy and self-determination. We hope that some of the overarching themes will serve to illustrate what we believe to be themes that resonate with many Indigenous groups. It is recognized that most of our readers will be familiar with the concepts presented here, so we make no pretense of presenting something new, but rather as a reminder of the context in which we are working.

A COMMUNITY VISION FOR CHILD WELFARE

The most important message from the community gatherings in the *Making our Hearts Sing* project was that the incorporation of cultural practices that support important familial and community kinship systems is critical to a process of recovery.[2] For this to occur, however, there are two prerequisites;

1. **Canada and the Provinces must own their responsibility to change legislation and funding in ways that reduce the impact of colonial policies on Aboriginal communities, families, and children, and allow for a higher degree of self-determination in charting their collective future.**

2. **Aboriginal people must intensify their awareness of the depth of colonization and its impact on their communities, especially on the children and youth who remain at high risk. Unless these are confronted, the disconnection from Aboriginal beliefs and values and the resulting devaluing of their child rearing and human development practices will continue to be perpetuated.**

An approach to child welfare consistent with Aboriginal culture would focus on family and collective human relationships. It would support a collective approach to child care responsibilities; an approach that encompasses the cultural continuity of a people.

---

[2]   The full report on the Making our Heart Sing Project is available under the title Leadership Forums in Alberta and can be accessed at http://www.cecw-cepb.ca/node/607

Cultural continuity is the cornerstone for the amelioration of the most negative and destructive impacts of colonization. These essential elements must be supported to interrupt the cycles of lateral violence in First Nations communities.

MAJOR THEMES

The major themes that emerged from the Making our Hearts Sing gatherings express the cultural and societal crisis of the community, as well as the community's understanding of what path needs to be followed on a successful journey toward recovery from this crisis.

These themes are:

1. **The Recovery and Affirmation of Cultural and a Way of Life**

   This involves a focus on identity and relationships, along with an understanding of the interconnectedness of language and the teachings of the Elders. The passing on of stories, which carry the knowledge of a people and the importance of kinship systems, are important components of responsibility for child care, socialization, and education.

2. **The Structural Violence of Colonial Policies and Practice:**

   The second theme reflects the realities of Aboriginal peoples' lived experience with colonial violence; the structural violence of poverty, marginalization, unemployment, and racism, with the added issues of substance abuse and lateral violence amongst family and community members.

1. RECOVERY AND AFFIRMATION OF CULTURE AND A WAY OF LIFE

a. *Making a path for children so that they can live fully.*

The cultural identity of the tribe is the most significant component in revitalizing and affirming traditional methods of child care. The separation and disconnection of people from the essence of their existence has been the most profound impact of residential schools and child welfare systems, as unity and wholeness of all parts of the Universe is at the heart of Aboriginal peoples' connection to their cultural and social identity.

The community shared that the teachings and stories must once again be told to the children, and that "our children must know who they are". The children must be given their cultural names; this is what connects them with the universe, the land, their community, spirituality, and family. Most importantly, this is what provides children with a place from which to securely participate in the world as they draw on the kinship relations from which their names are derived. Reuniting and affirming these relational connections and the responsibilities imbued in these relationships is the essential function of cultural and social identity.

The stories must be told in the original language. Language reflects the philosophical system of the people and evokes a relational perspective which mirrors their sacred world (Bastien, 2004). It reflects the meanings ascribed to existence, the purpose of relationships, and the responsibilities inherent in these connections. It provides a way of interpreting the world in which children live (Bastien, 2004). Language guides the epistemology and pedagogical practices of the tribe; it is instrumental in creating knowledge and creating reality (Bastien, 2004). New responsibilities, organizational structures, programs, and services can flow from this connection to traditional knowledge and the responsibilities of the collective. Inclusion and connection are integral to the way of life and identity of Indigenous people and can inform the development of new programs and services. More specifically, participants stressed the importance of revisiting Indigenous education by:

- Incorporating Indigenous methods of research
- Recording and documenting traditional knowledge
- Rethinking educational programs
- Involving the community in changing the social environment
- Making language education mandatory
- Educating young parents, linking them with Elders and positive role models

b. *Collective recovery through participating in Indigenous culture.*

The disruption to Aboriginal family and community life is evident as the effects of colonization, specifically residential school, has continued with the current approach to child welfare service delivery. In order to be effective, this approach must be consistent with Aboriginal values, which include affirming attachment to family and community life, parental bonding, kindness, and nurturing children with love and acceptance. Recent Western scientific findings about the nature of reality reveal that everything is related to everything else in the universe; this knowledge is not new to Indigenous people who have always understood the universe to be the indivisible whole that quantum physics now understands. This indivisible wholeness of the universe is the source of Aboriginal spirituality. The cultural principles and assumptions of Aboriginality, a way of life based on spirituality as the source of all relationships, calls upon all people to assume responsibility for all relationships.

c. *Indigenous Human Development Approach.*

An Indigenous human development approach based on collective responsibilities must guide the development of programs and services for families and children. It must begin with those who are most vulnerable and who contain the greatest hope for a new era for Aboriginal people; the children.

Here is a summary of what an Indigenous Human Development Approach could include:

- Use of language; this is a medium through which speakers can call into existence a world of relationships and alliances.
- Stories; these are the foundation of knowledge, as well as the foundation of inclusiveness and harmony.
- Children to be taught about ancestors, history, and alliances through language, stories, and ceremony.
- Integrating tribal ways into everyday life.
- Coming together in gatherings, feasts, and ceremonies.
- Focusing on the wisdom of the Elders; connecting youth and Elders.
- Following practices that support and affirm a more spiritual way of life.

- Using strategies that are guided by traditional principles of collective responsibility.
- Social workers trained in Aboriginal culture and community awareness, including the history and effects of colonization.

2. STRUCTURAL VIOLENCE OF COLONIAL POLICIES AND PRACTICE

A belief in power and control has been central to the mastery of one culture over another. Colonialism has made Indigenous nations dependent by stripping them of their own resources, their means of economic sustainability, and their ways of knowledge production, leaving a legacy of abuse and violence that rendered them powerless and demoralized.

This violence terrorizes and re-traumatizes communities with programs structured on the very tenents of genocide; hierarchy, paternalism, patriarchy, power, control, racism, rationality, and empiricism. These tenents continue to fragment and isolate individuals, leaving communities hopeless and in despair.

Aboriginal communities in Canada continue to rank near the bottom of the United Nations quality of life index, while other Canadians are positioned near the top (Blackstock & Bennett, 2002). Poverty, inadequate housing, and substance abuse are leading factors for child welfare involvement and must be addressed if significant gains are to be achieved (Blackstock & Trocmé, 2005).

It is essential for local, provincial and federal authorities to acknowledge the importance of community views in policy and program development for these issues to be addressed effectively, and community members call for urgent collaboration and community action on the following issues:

- Fundamental systemic factors, such as poverty and inadequate housing, as these are priority issues for improving the health of the community.
- Aboriginal men's loss of self-respect and a valued place in the community. Healing, employment, and other means of improving self-sufficiency are essential for Aboriginal men to take their place in creating a strong community.
- Lateral and family violence and increasing rates of alcohol abuse are critical issues that need to be addressed effectively and in a culturally appropriate manner.
- Children lost to the community through adoption. The creation of laws to protect the children who have been adopted outside the community and to develop longer term foster care solutions and finding better ways of keeping their children connected.
- The growth of gang violence is increasingly worrisome.
- Ineffective child welfare programs requires increased parental involvement in planning more responsive child welfare programs.
- The health and well-being of the Elders who are said to be dying at the rate of one per week in a community that depends upon them to pass on values, history, and tradition. This is critical to the future of the community and to the formation of culturally appropriate programs and services.

REFLECTIONS

1. How can we best work with Elders and ceremonialists in the construction of knowledge systems, conceptual frameworks and pedagogy for social work practice based on cultural integrity?

2. How do we proceed to develop new program models based on community guidance that will be in harmony with the Aboriginal way of life and inform a new legislative framework?

3. How can we evaluate existing models that offer promise for broader application?

4. How can we establish demonstration projects to affirm and evaluate the community recommendations?

5. How can we develop curriculum for First Nations social work leadership and organizational change?

6. How can we develop training programs for human services workers working with First Nations communities that pursue cultural continuity as their primary objective?

7. What can each of us do to create greater understanding and shared goals to ensure a brighter future for Aboriginal children?

SOURCES

Blackstock, C., & Bennett, M. (2002). *Affirming and promoting Indigenous knowledge and research.* Unpublished presentation. Centre of Excellence for Child Welfare and First Nations Child & Family Caring Society of Canada.

Blackstock, C., & Trocmé, N. (2005). Community based child welfare for Aboriginal children: Supporting resilience through structural change. In M. Ungar (Ed.), *Pathways to resilience: A Handbook of theory, methods and interventions* (pp.105-120). Thousand Oaks, CA: Sage Publication.

We are grateful to the communities of the Blood Tribe (Kainai Nation), the Sturgeon Lake Cree Nation, and the Métis Settlements for their generosity in sharing their vision for the future. We consider ourselves blessed to have benefited from their wisdom. A special thanks to Rosie Day Rider, Nina Scout and Andy Blackwater from the Blood Tribe; Mary Kappo and Margaret Kappo, and Jerry Goodswimmer from Sturgeon Lake for their friendship and support.

I wish to acknowledge the following persons for their contributions to the process:

From the Blood Reserve: Betty Bastien, Susan Bare Shin Bone, Robin Little Bear, Kim Gravelle and Lance Tailfeathers.

From Sturgeon Lake: David Nabew, Leroy Hamelin, and Alvina Nabew

From the Métis Child and Family Services Region of ACYS: Shane Gauthier, Shannon Souray and Lillian Parenteau.

From the Creating Hope Gathering; Sharon Shirt, Martha Ouellette, Herb Lehr and Bernadette Iahtail for sharing their experience for our film.

Finally I wish to acknowledge my colleagues Betty Bastien, Ralph Bodor and Jessica Ayala, who collaborated in the production of the monograph upon which this is based. It is entitled *Leadership Forums in Aboriginal Child welfare: Making our Hearts Sing and is available on line on the Center of Excellence for Child welfare at http://www.cecw-cepb.ca/catalogue.*

Chapter 6

Persons Who Have Been In Care

Key points

1. We need to pay attention to the experiences of those who have been in care as they have important lessons to teach us.
2. These include lessons of resilience in the face of hardship, of forgiveness and at times of gratitude.
3. In spite of their difficulties they offer us hope that we can do better by them, their children and grandchildren.

In November of 2006, the Creating Hope Society of Alberta hosted a gathering, *Creating Hope for the Future* in Edmonton, Alberta. It was a gathering of Aboriginal persons who were in the care of the child welfare system for a significant period of their lives. The setting was very powerful as survivors of the child welfare system shared their experiences with each other and child welfare workers who were prepared to learn from these experiences.

The following describes some key themes that emerged from the gathering, as told in the voices of those who experienced the child welfare system first hand. This is followed by an explanation of some basic elements of a course that has been created based upon these experiences. In no way does this claim to represent the feelings of all Aboriginal children who have been in care, but it is considered to be an accurate representation of the views of the 160 persons who attended the first such gathering.

I hope that it will allow us to pause and consider the longer term impacts of our decisions to place children into care situations, and reflect more deeply on the options that we offer to families and the child welfare workers who are dedicated to their service.

KEY THEMES FROM THE GATHERING

THEME 1: FAILURE OF THE SYSTEM

The child welfare system has been damaging to Aboriginal people.

- The current child welfare system continues to cause damage by neglecting to consider the full and proper kinship of families, refusing to look at how we as Native people live, how our homes are places of love, caring, sharing, and teaching.
- What happened to us when we were very young is still happening to us today; we are still losing our children.
- Native children need to be in their own community if they must go into foster care or adoption.
- There is insufficient funding available to enable Aboriginal communities to set up their own systems.
- There is still a lack of trust by Aboriginal people toward the child welfare system.

- The uncertainty of family background because of the way children were taken away can make it difficult to know family members very well.
- The child welfare systems have been driven and controlled by "white society" and "white society" values.
- The child welfare system is changing, but there is still the need to make it work better for us.

THEME 2: LIVING WITH THE PAST

We must continue to deal with the pain and anger of the past, even as we try to move on.

- Feeling abandoned and betrayed with no connection to my birth community.
- Feeling robbed of childhood, feeling deep sadness of not having shared how our spirits died in this process and fear for the future.
- Feeling the betrayal of trust because many of us ended up in situations where we were unable to go back to our birth community yet unable to leave an abusive situation in the foster/adoptive home.
- Finding ways to get beyond anger and learning how to trust, to forgive those who hurt us.
- The pain of continuing to see parents and children going through the same issues.
- Never feeling part of any family or community; never experiencing what it is like to love and be loved.
- Feeling shame in being Aboriginal in a white society.
- Find that so many parts of life are "not whole".

THEME 3: SHARING THE JOURNEY

We are finding strength and hope from each other in sharing the journey to healing.

- It is a long, never-ending journey, but you are not alone.
- Coming to acceptance of what happened with birth parents, with the child welfare system, with foster and adoptive families so that we can move on.
- Getting through the sadness, the abuse, the feeling of being deserted by my spirituality, the unfairness of society expecting people who went through this kind of trauma to function like other people.
- The problems of living out the bad memories of the past in finding healing, to face an ocean of sadness, tears never cried, feeling that no one cared.
- Forgiving our biological parents, our foster and adoptive parents.
- Learning different ways to come to terms with life; learning things in life to help with the journey.

THEME 4: BELONGING SOMEWHERE

We are discovering who we are, where we belong and to whom we belong.

- Developing an understanding that "I am not alone"; that I belong somewhere.
- Overcoming the "not knowing" where you belong and the sense of total abandonment.

- Growing up not knowing how to have healthy relationships: the problems with intimacy and relationships and the ease of staying "distant" because of the abuse, lack of love and isolation from a caring family or community.
- Hurt has come from both the Aboriginal and non-Aboriginal side: finding that the Aboriginal community would not accept me, and how draining life can be.
- Discomfort in trying to live on a reserve.
- Discovering and learning about culture, ceremonies, and community.
- Reuniting with biological parents and siblings, sometimes very positive, sometimes painful and unsuccessful.

THEME 5: TOWARD HEALING

The Gathering offered the opportunity to reconnect: to feel it, live it, use it as a milestone on the journey to healing.

- Feeling proud of being native, passing this pride on to my own children.
- Believing I am here for a reason, to give back to my people.
- Discovering spirituality and affirmation of being a worthwhile person.
- Coming to accept who I am.
- Wanting to thank my adoptive parents for the good that they did, for the love that was there, values and ethics they gave me; a lot of what we learned in the places we were raised was positive.

- We have learned much even in the pain through which we have lived.
- The joy of being reconnected (at the Gathering): feeling it, learning it, living it; finding we are not alone (i.e. what is happening today, discovering that everything I went through brought me here, and that this experience is a stepping-stone).
- The need to create hope for so many people who do not know there is life after hell.
- Feeling proud of the people at the Gathering for being strong and coming as part of a learning journey, sharing their stories. From listening today, I have hope.
- Happiness in being here (at the Gathering) and the sharing; finding a way to reach out and trust (try to trust) people.
- Needing to break the silence (at the Gathering).
- Knowing there is a Creator and that calling on the Creator provides hope and strength.

WHAT CAN WE DO WITH SUCH DIFFICULT ISSUES?

The themes you have just read and the stories they were derived from are painful ones. They are as powerful and profound as they are tragic. We must embrace them with an open mind and an open heart, which will then allow us to face them without shutting down or jumping too quickly to find solutions. For that process, we look to the genius and brilliance of Indigenous ways of life and worldviews for finding the best way possible to put our hearts and minds together to see what we can do about this. Sadly, we now realize that many of the outcomes of child welfare interventions have been tragic. It is to us all, now, to have the courage required to look at those results and determine what went wrong.

I wish to acknowledge the Creating Hope Society for creating a forum for 160 persons who had live their childhood in the care of the child welfare system. Their testimonials were powerful and motivating to improve our services based upon their life experience. It would take another book to describe the richness of their sharing. While this short summary cannot do justice to the pathos and pain that they have experience, we must appreciate their courage and willingness to share and support one another.

Chapter 7

Professional Staff Perspectives: The Bent Arrow Traditional Healing Society & Alberta Child and Youth Services

Key points

1. The chapter describes the benefits of placing non-Aboriginal staff in an Aboriginal agency, the Bent Arrow Traditional Healing Society, which is immersed in traditional approaches.
2. Three points are made by a group of front-line, supervisory and managerial staff about important considerations for practice:
    a. The importance of relationship as the fundamental component for practice.
    b. The yearning of workers for increased opportunities to exercise creativity in their practice and the extent to which they struggle with the constraints imposed by the policies and procedures under which they must operate.
    c. What they need from leadership if these are to be possible for them.

In John Ralston Saul's recent book, *A Fair Country*, he declares that Canada is a Métis country, in light of four hundred years of Aboriginal people rubbing shoulders with non-Aboriginal settlers. He suggests that this interaction has shaped our national identity, and that Aboriginal values have shaped who we are in ways that we have yet to fully realize. The Bent Arrow co-location project mirrors in many ways what Saul suggests, with similar benefits for this entity. The following description will elaborate on this perspective. This collaboration was intended to explore the experience of co-locating a staff unit from the Children and Youth Services Ministry with the Bent Arrow Healing Society. We were interested in learning what this experience would have to teach us about the impact of being immersed in an urban Aboriginal agency and how it might alter the perspective of non-Aboriginal professional staff accustomed to working in a traditional government office. Staff from Alberta Children's Services and Bent Arrow met monthly over a 9 month period, using a Participatory Action Research approach with two researchers from the Faculty of Social Work. As the process unfolded, we learned a great deal about how the practice world appeared to both government and agency staff. This chapter discusses two elements of our learning. The first is the impact for non-Aboriginal staff working in an Aboriginal setting. The second is the identification of some key elements of social work practice that were important to the child welfare staff that participated.

WHAT IS IT LIKE FOR NON-ABORIGINAL STAFF TO WORK IN AN ABORIGINAL SETTING?

As will be clear from reading the following transcripts, there was a great deal of enthusiasm about working in this setting. Our initial interest was in exploring how non-Aboriginal professional child welfare workers placed in an Aboriginal agency that followed traditional Aboriginal approaches to practice might change their orientation to their work and to Aboriginal people generally. Bent Arrow differs from most local office settings in the following ways;

- It is located in an older building that does not have all of the high security characteristic of a modern child welfare office
- Clients can access the building freely, including the common coffee room
- Each day begins with a prayer and a smudge
- Meals are a source of celebration, where staff and clients come together
- The agency is very much a part of its community and noted for creating innovative programs that are responsive to community needs
- There is a strong spirit of collegiality and laughter present in the hallways and work areas.

THE EXPERIENCE OF CO-LOCATION; IN THE WORDS OF THE WORKERS

We all have common ground somewhere so I just deal with people on a one-to-one kind of basis. I think it's very cool in the differences in the way you approach practice. The co-location projects let you get stuff done, people are right there, you see them daily, hourly, sometimes they're just there eight hours a day. I don't like the whole way government offices are set up. I think we need to be very cautious as a society, that we don't destroy our ability to form relationships and our ability to interact with people on every level because that is, in essence, our humanity and if we strip that from ourselves, we lose so much more than what we've already lost. Different cultures, I think, are even secondary to the fact that we're all human; we all have the same basic needs for belonging, for nurturing and to ensure that this is intact.

I feel freer to bring my clients here. In a government office . . . We're always behind closed doors. The physical space is so different here, that it's more inviting. It helps my practice just by being here.

Yeah, there's a lot of issues . . . historical issues because of the oppression and there's trust issues. I had to look within my own belief system and say, "I can share my experience on what my work is doing so far here in this organization, with the community and families and I have a lot to share on that subject. Culturally and spiritually, that's how I can make sense of my world and my life and my being. When I see things through the spiritual sense, that's when everything becomes clearer for me.

When you have workers and supervisors working with community agencies and the actual families under one roof or in one very small area, you get to understand the perspective of the families, the geographic location, the ethnicities that live in that location and so if you can get a perspective that the families are coming from, then you provide better service to those families.

WHAT GOVERNMENT STAFF LOVE ABOUT BENT ARROW

- We learn to share common goals
- We can embrace a different culture

- We get know each other at a more human level
- The community becomes a mirror that challenges our belief systems
- We belong to the community
- We connect with the community in a manner that shares culture and respects our differences
- We can discover our similarities
- We learn about our common beliefs
- We can laugh together

CORE CONCEPTS DERIVED
FROM THE GROUP PROCESS

Three concepts were fundamental to the learning that emerged from this process. These are the importance of the *relationship* between social workers and those they serve, with each other, with the different levels of the organization and with the community. Aligned with this is the concept of *creativity*. Staff yearns for the opportunity to be more innovative in their responses to client situations and feels hemmed in by rigid policies, procedures and limited service options that are not always responsive to clients' problems. Lastly, there is a plea for supportive and understanding *leadership* at all levels of the organization, and for the willingness to not only permit, but to encourage leadership at the front line that makes the fullest use of their ideas and experiences.

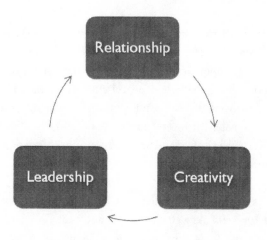

CORE CONCEPT 1—RELATIONSHIP

Workers felt that **the importance of relationship is not given due to consideration** in policy, planning, administration, service delivery, or quality assurance. The current reality is that time demands take away from developing relationship, committees take away from connecting with families on your caseload, and new practice models take away from focus on the family. In other words, procedural things get in the way of relationships.

They hope that **a greater focus on relationship would improve working relationships** at all levels. It was felt that an improved understanding leads to better planning and better service. A multi-disciplinary approach (more minds, experience, and perspectives taking part in problem-solving and service planning) would be of mutual benefit to Children's Services and Agencies and would add credibility with community.

This would call for the reduction of barriers and the removal of the fear of retribution for mistakes. This co-location maximized opportunities to develop relationships. It was hoped that at the individual level clients should have improved access to social workers and would view them in a more supportive role. Ultimately, families and communities will be better served and the Ministry and community agencies work more effectively together.

Workers expressed the belief that the **information that goes to the top gets skewed**, distorted, and that only bad stories come to light (case reviews). Often, when senior people visit worksites, everything 'shines', but the truth of everyday practice lies somewhere in the middle. They believe that their leaders do not value and support the importance of their relationships with clients and each other. There is a great **need for support from leadership** and a greater buy-in from staff who may have lost sight of the importance of this concept

At a systemic level, contrary to the prevailing workplace ideology with its emphasis on rigid timelines and limited availability to contain costs, workers believe that **recognition of the importance of relationship would make better use of resources**; less money will be pumped into the system, and social workers will have greater job satisfaction.

Their ultimate vision is for improved outcomes for families, increased stability at all levels of the organization, a revised definition of successful family stories, and everyone (workers and families) will be treated with greater respect.

Group Narratives on Relationship

It was very clear to me, the importance of relationship and really getting to know the youth . . . you get to know them so well and in a short time they didn't't care whether you were from child welfare or what your authority was. They just wanted connection and they wanted relationship.

The other thing was being connected to the community and [realizing] how little we're able to accomplish when we're working in isolation. Most of the time, we can default to community problem solving, bringing in resources and building relationships with the youth. These are much more effective tools and if none of those work, then we can take that next step.

I work in a unit of high risk youth; we focus on building relationships and a harm reduction resiliency philosophy, but we also use secure services, along the continuum of harm reduction it is sometimes intrusive in order to keep the youth safe. I hope the difference is that because we already have strongly established relationships with the youth . . . that they're okay being there.

We're finding too, that . . . we know the youth so well, they're talking to us lots and they're talking about some of their childhood trauma experiences and aside from them having to continue to live with that, it has an effect on us as well, as it does all workers.

. . . (Relationship) is just taking us back to why we've gone into the field. It's so very basic and simple. It's to build relationships, and ultimately, it's a very simple concept. I really keep hearing about connection and relationship and . . . you're reminding me why I became a social worker many years ago. It was because of that relationship, working with the children, the family, the youth, not worrying about a thousand overdue things.

Yeah, the science is finding that relationship, how we make that change, by having good relationships with people, by engaging with them, that is how we make change. Yet we're introducing more technology and taking that relationship building away. How are we going to do a better job? Paperwork might be more up-to-date but how are we actually going to make appreciable change?

After eighteen years of being on the front lines, I think that in all relationships with kids you need the ability to connect, establish rapport, and engage with them . . . you can make jokes, you can talk to them. In other words, just being real should not intimidate you.

I'm a very relationship focused person; there are families that I served eight years ago and I still remember who grandma is because I developed a relationship so I know who they're talking about. You can chitchat and glean information in the most amazing ways. I was out yesterday to meet one of my mom's; she had made her sister come in from Spruce Grove 'because her sister wanted to meet me'. I think that was great.

Organizational pre-requisites for healthy relationships

- Supportive peers
- Supportive agencies
- Support from supervisor
- Flexible supervision—need to be flexible from both ends
- Respect for each other
- Time together
- Challenge pre-conceptions and assumptions
- Establish trust between clients and worker
- Respect our differences
- Trust between organizational levels
- Openness
- Rapport based
- Keep it real
- Trust in partners

REFLECTIONS

If relationship was the most important consideration in our work:

- Would our offices not be more client-friendly?
- Would we not value a receptive environment more than exaggerated security?
- Would we not eliminate such 'safety 'constraints as cipher locks and shatterproof panels?
- Would we not question what message our work settings are sending to the children, the families and the community?

- Would we not ask why we consider our children and families so dangerous?
- Would we ask why we spend so much precious time at computer screens?

If relationship was the most important consideration in our <u>program delivery</u>:

- Would we not find more creative ways to keep families together and keep children safe?
- Would we still place children hundreds of miles away from their communities and families?
- Would so many children still lose their connection to siblings, parents, grandparents and extended family?
- Would professional staff be so unavailable to the children in their care?
- Would there be so many specialists in the lives of children, few of whom create continuity?
- Would children have so many different foster homes?
- Would child welfare workers' relationships with children and families be as easily disrupted for *administrative* reasons?
- Would siblings placed in the same city remain isolated from each other?
- Would so many fathers lose their connection to their children and families?
- Would so many children spend their lives in care and end up on the streets and in jail?

If relationship was the most important consideration <u>with kin and community</u>:

- Would not all children know their relatives and keep in contact with them?
- Would the community not see its children as its responsibility?
- Would we not find more creative ways to sustain connections to family and community, for example homecoming celebrations?
- Would we not create a more positive relationship with the community?
- Would we not find better ways to recognize and support kinship connections?
- Would we not more fully support Aboriginal families of children in care in sharing their values?
- Would we not ensure that Aboriginal children and their parents learn the family ways of grandparents, parents, aunts' uncles, cousins, and other extended family?

CORE CONCEPT 2—CREATIVITY

Workers felt that the bureaucratic system is too rigid to allow for positive creativity from both the workers and the families. It is their hope that we can create a system that is less rigid and focuses more on children and their families. This in turn would create a happier and healthier worker who can better support families to be happy and healthier.

They believe that we need **increased communication at all levels.** This calls for greater openness and a willingness to negotiate. An important dimension is the achievement of increased trust between senior and mid-management, along with a willingness to recognize the skills of frontline workers. There is a need to acknowledge that many of their decisions are calculated risks, that sometimes bad things happen and not to react so strongly to them. Many feel overwhelmed by administrative duties and become bogged down with approval requirements on relatively minor decisions that are a drain on precious time that could be better spent with our families. They believe that such changes can benefit children, families, workers, leadership teams, policy makers, and legal staff.

While there is a need for resources to achieve greater creativity, they feel that **we can make much better use of existing resources if there is a receptivity to change**. In their view we need people willing to champion creativity, an organization that recognizes its importance, and flexible funding that lends itself to experimentation. Management needs to communicate that this is an acceptable path to a more satisfying career track. It is essential to create an open environment for listening and negotiating between management and front-line staff, and greater transparency in our communications. We need more feedback on the outcomes of our efforts with clients, and to feel valued and respected for our work. Creativity can be encouraged with meaningful rewards that are determined in consultation with each other. Finally, room for creativity will allow for a more evenly distributed leadership that can involve all of us in the creation of a more flexible and creative service system. We will have happier and healthier families and diminished staff turnover as a result of greater job satisfaction. This should result in a reduction of dependence on additional resources. We can anticipated the development of more self-directed staff who feel empowered and ultimately a more self-sustaining service system that can be of greater service to families and enhance the overall image of the Ministry.

The ultimate vision is for an effective service system that is focused on meaningful interventions and collaboration with families and their communities, and that all levels of the Ministry will be open to a new way of practice; that workers will be open to new and creative thinking and be encouraged to think outside the box. It is suggested that other agencies with whom we collaborate are also open to creativity, but that it is important that the total organization demonstrate a willingness to tolerate managed risk.

Group Narratives on Creativity

I started to see a pattern evolving and the part that really bothered me was that it seemed every time there was some kind of crisis that got media attention, the response invariably was to try and nail things down a bit tighter. This trend has continued leaving less freedom, less room for creativity and room for movement. So that is part of my bias and I worry about it because I think it takes away from what we're doing with clients; we end up depriving clients of things because of this reactive mode.

. . . The group spirit is infectious when you're around a bunch of people who want to do different service and be creative. It lights a spark in your own creativity that will allow you to develop further creativity, whereas if you're in an environment that's not that conducive to thinking outside the box and trying new things, it deadens that flame.

Trying to be creative in an environment that doesn't't really foster this has been a challenge for me, whereas in the Inner City Connections Unit, taking the parent along when you're apprehending their child, to do the intake, and foster home placement is a part of the process and doesn't't really confuse anybody. At the Millwoods office, it threw them for a loop the first time I took a parent on the apprehension with me. Who does that?

I guess one of the things that hit home is how we react to crises by making things tighter. It is stifling when that happens. Every time you turn around, there's more paper . . . I know we have to be accountable but sometimes the paperwork and the timelines take away from our work with our clients. This morning a client came to meet me; her agreement is ending. One of her concerns was that it's ending when we just started to see some success. How can you think of closing it? We're not even there yet, but that's already . . . on the table.

There is truth in the specifics. The policy makers are trying to globalize rules to fit every situation, when what really needs to happen is to look at the specifics of the truth. For example, the school policy is that a teacher or staff cannot give a child a hug if they scrape their knee. Applying this in real life seems ridiculous and less than human. Global rules clearly cannot be made to fit every situation.

If you give training to people to be helpers frame it like "Here are some generic tools, along with your own skills. Use them to do the job we hired you to do, because you possess the skills you need and you are going to adapt them to the specifics . . . because there are a million of them!"

REFLECTIONS

If creativity were paramount:

- Would leadership look askance at those who push the envelope?
- Would we keep being weighed down with ever increasing information requirements?
- Would top down direction keep shifting as new programs are created?
- Would front line staff and managers not be granted the freedom to respond in a more flexible fashion to the needs and strengths of their communities and families?
- Would the procedural bounds that contain our creativity not be loosened?
- Would we not listen to our clients, foster parents, associate agencies, and community members and learn from them what is working and what is not?
- Would we not engage clients in finding new solutions to our problems?
- Would we not share our reality with those who can assist us with fresh ideas and perspectives?
- Would we not allow for mistakes to be made in the interest of learning?

CORE CONCEPT 3—LEADERSHIP

There is a sense that senior leadership has lost touch with front line needs; the system allows only for an overriding concern with optics and political considerations. At the mid-management level, leadership is failing to connect or set the tone because of onerous policy and paper work demands. This is creating a sense of chaos in the system and it is restricting the capacity to meet commitments. According to participants, there is a lack of solid/effective leadership; this is largely attributable to an over-emphasis on cost effectiveness rather than families, and on form filling over meaningful casework.

It is recommended that senior leadership regain a focus on what is 'real' and truly needed for the front line. This includes closing the gap between ideal standards and day-to-day operations. Staff invites their senior and mid-level leaders to reconnect with them and to support them, and help set the tone to better assist families; their priority should be on supporting healthy relationships and freeing workers for more creative work.

Workers suggested that minimal funds would be needed to make such a change. It calls for a shift in thinking and the establishment of priorities; In the long run, such action would actually save dollars by reducing staff turnover and burnout.

An improved connection with workers would lead to happier workers and better served families. Ultimately, this would create a more effective, well supported and happier team. At a systemic level workers could work in a more optimistic fashion, if they were freed to focus on what they are trained to do as social workers. They hope that their work lives would not feel so lost and cluttered. Our most important goal is to be able to do our work without fear, but rather with the freedom to be creative and to empower the families with whom we work.

In making these recommendations, they recognize that they may be difficult to acknowledge, but from their vantage point, leadership needs to shift as they seems, at this time, to be stuck. In their words:

We believe that this kind of change can have a positive impact and that our leaders will be capable of this change when they see the legitimacy of our perspective. We hope that our leaders will not hesitate in making such changes as a result of political pressures and expectations. We believe that this can be an effective strategy to address some of the issues that have bedeviled the ministry for many years.

What we need to know will be made visible by the action of our Minister and the willingness of our leaders; this will filter down to front line workers, and the shift will be felt by workers and families. We will know that it has happened when we feel like more effective and connected front line workers; when the tenor of the organization is freer and when we feel more supported, less frustrated, and more able to be flexible with families.

Group Narratives on Leadership

Well, I think that our leaders, if they are going to be working in Children's Services, should be required to spend some time each year in a group home or foster home to better know the children that we are serving. I think there needs to be some sort of a mandatory element of exposure to the front line so that they can more fully understand some of the issues we must address.

Shawna Seneca, (Co-founder and executive director of Bent Arrow) taught me that the ability to have a mentor and the ability to be a mentor is really critically important in this field because the people in our lives made . . . it's been just over a year since she passed away and she was such a strong mentor that without realizing it over the years I've sponged up the things she's taught me and I portray those traits in my day to day practice. In doing so, I have become mentor to many of the Bent Arrow staff. If we can perpetuate that philosophy, we can teach the next generation of social workers that we can get something done eventually. We see how jaded and unhelpful some social workers can be, and we want this next generation of social workers and helpers to remember why they wanted to help people.

What I'd like to see from policy makers is a non-punitive approach when things don't go right. The analogy I use is that of an emergency room triage. We have all these files coming in, they're all high-risk kids, and they're all high-risk families. Sometimes things go bad and it's not because of bad practice, it's not because we have bad policies, it's not because of anything that we have done specifically. When you look at an emergency room in a hospital, if a patient dies, it doesn't mean the doctor did anything wrong. He's not punished and there's no punitive process in place. There may be a review to see if things can be improved, but generally, you don't hear of doctors being punished if a patient dies. In our practice if something goes wrong with the family, everybody looks at the case manager and then their supervisor to see what they didn't do, what policies they didn't adhere to, if the paperwork is up-to-date. This is a very punitive kind of approach when things go bad; we're dealing with high-risk families, we're dealing with high-risk kids and sometimes those risks become insurmountable in certain situations. I would like . . . policy makers to know that we deal with high risk people, and that it's not always going to turn out well.

Group discussion on Leadership

- There is no way to teach potential social workers every possible scenario they are going to encounter. Yet we can create a new policy over one terrible incident.
- Currently there is a very punitive approach when things go bad when working with high risk families.
- We need to look at social work practice like Emergency Room Triage. All files are 'at risk' families. If things go bad, it's not necessarily bad practice; it was a bad situation but we did our best to manage it.
- If a patient dies in the emergency room, it may be because his injuries were beyond anyone's ability to help; when someone dies in social work, we automatically turn the focus on what the caseworker or supervisor did wrong, what standards were not met.
- It takes courage to do what is right in social work. Policy makers need the courage to implement policies that say 'we are going to do what is right' rather than smoothing things over. *Adapt to the specifics and do what's right rather than just doing everything politically correctly.*

REFLECTIONS

If leadership were valued from all levels in the organization would we not?

- Have more joint decision-making?
- Have a commitment to make it work at all levels?
- Have a greater sincerity and genuine interest in each other's points of view?
- Have a greater willingness to listen to each other?
- Create a win—win environment, as opposed to a "cover your ass" mentality?
- Have respect for wisdom born of experience?
- Be focused and committed to the team?
- Allow natural leaders to lead, and not only those in the hierarchy?
- Allow all people to shine, including children, families and communities?

DISCUSSION

It seems clear that this group of social workers has benefited from working in an Aboriginal setting and that it has had a positive effect on their practice. The months of reflection on practice issues has provided them with an opportunity to think about what is important about their practice as social workers, and how the organizational environment contributes to or detracts from this.

It also seems clear that the current child welfare paradigm does not fully meet their expectations, and that they would love to have the opportunity to more fully engage in meaningful relationships with the children and families they work with; to be granted more freedom and creativity in how they respond to them, to receive more supportive leadership while being encouraged to provide leadership in their own roles as caseworkers, supervisors, family support workers, and administrative staff.

The staff has been articulate about the **impediments to achieving this vision**:

1. Undue emphasis on paper processing,
2. Rigid procedures,
3. The encroachment of technology that does not serve them well,
4. Complicated approval levels for relatively minor decisions,
5. A work environment that is too often governed by fear.

These impediments lead to a lack of honesty between the various levels in the hierarchy and reluctance to express one's truth in a more forthright manner. This is a very dangerous situation for any organization.

While we cannot be sure that all social workers feel the same way, it is suggested that these themes are worth exploring further. This takes courage on the part of any organization, and especially on the part of one that has been the subject of such vociferous public criticism over the past three decades.

While it may be of little comfort, Alberta is not alone in this situation. Many of our Canadian, American, and Australian Child welfare services have suffered the same fate, especially with regard to serving Aboriginal people.

For the most part, with relatively minor variations, we are all pursuing the same path, which is leading us to make some important gains. But there is much to do, and we hope that the perspective of this small band of social workers who have come together in the Bent Arrow Healing Society will help us to realize that we are likely to find a better way by coming together as brothers and sisters who share the same human and spiritual ideals.

SOURCES

Linda Kreitzer (my colleague and co-investigator) and I are grateful to the staff and administration of the Bent Arrow Traditional Healing Society for allowing us an opportunity to dialogue with their staff for over a year.

We wish to especially acknowledge Shauna Seneca, with whom we commenced discussing this possibility, and sadly passed away just prior to beginning work on this initiative. Cheryl Whiskeyjack was pressed into service as executive director, and graciously not only supported our efforts, but participated in all of our sessions with Bent Arrow and government staff. We wish to thank the 9 workers who took time from their busy lives to reflect on a monthly basis on their work and the context in which it was performed. And finally we wish to thank our advisory committee of Ministry staff were so generous with their time and advice.

Chapter 8

Synchronicity or Serendidipity: Aboriginal Wisdom and Resilient Children

Key Points

1. There are interesting possibilities in comparing Aboriginal wisdom with current concepts about childhood resiliency.
2. Perhaps we can create greater understanding between us by using a common language that we can all understand.

Research suggests that there may be a high level of congruence between Aboriginal worldviews and modern theories of childhood resilience. A number of Aboriginal writers have recently focused on aspects of resiliency that resonate with the cultural solutions advocated by their Elders (Blackstock & Trocme, 2004; Laboucane-Benson 2005; Hunter and Lewis, 2006; and Dion-Stout, 2003). Laboucane-Benson (2005, p.7) states that "for Aboriginal families, a resilience framework must consider and reflect their worldview, including a need for balance, fluidity, and the interconnectedness of family members, the community, and the cosmos." She goes on to describe how during the research process for the Royal Commission on Aboriginal People, many Aboriginal people re-iterated that "families are at the core of the process of renewal in which they are engaged" (Canada, 1996b; p.1). The renewal process for Aboriginal families is a continuation of the resilience demonstrated by Aboriginal people's survival in the face of genocidal policies; in contemporary society there is evidence of inherent resilience. In a powerful testament to the resiliency of their people, two presenters from the Victoria Aboriginal Child Care Agency suggested that,

> *In order to have a positive future our children need to be resilient. Not only resilient to the past which is imprinted on their genes and the living memory of their parents, grandparents, families, and communities, but also resilient to a colonized environment which denigrates their very sense of identity and being. So many Aboriginal child and family service practitioners seek to build on the one positive fact for today's Aboriginal and Islander communities—we have survived: we have proved resilient* (Hunter and Lewis, 2006 ACWA Conference Presentation).

In his description of identity formation and cultural resilience in Aboriginal communities, Lalonde (2006) states that:

> *Resilience implies transcendence. While there is perhaps no happy ending to be found in the story told by these data, there is hope. Within a population that suffers the highest rate of suicide in any culturally identifiable group in the world, and that even after the "60s scoop" continues to see a disproportionate number of children taken into care, there is evidence of resilience. The surprising*

> *outcomes—the transcendence—is not found in the
> single 'hardy' or 'invulnerable' child who manages
> to rise above adversity, but in the existence of whole
> communities that demonstrate the power of culture
> as a protective factor. When communities succeed
> in promoting their cultural heritage and in securing
> control of their own collective future—in claiming
> ownership over their past and future; the positive
> effects reverberate across many measures of youth
> health and well-being* (p. 23).

Aboriginal communities are clear about the essential values and philosophy that must guide the development of programs and services. They include:

(1) Shared parenting,
(2) Community responsibility for children,
(3) The importance of language as a source of renewed culture,
(4) Knowledge of history and tradition as an essential element of identity,
(5) The importance of kinship and connection to each other,
(6) A respectful approach to all of life.

Aboriginal people hold a holistic view of the universe and seek to balance the physical, mental, emotional, and spiritual elements of life. Sharing and respect have been essential to survival for millennia.

Congruent with these aspects of Aboriginal culture, resilience theory describes protective factors that include;

(1) Having one person in life that values and respects the child (mentor/Elder),

(2) A connection to community (history/tradition),

(3) A connection to a church (spirituality),

(4) Healthy peer relationships (identity),

(5) Development of at least one talent or skill (traditional skills such as drumming/dancing),

(6) Contribution to one's community/school (being seen as part of the solution for one's people).

A more systematic application of both Aboriginal and resilience perspectives can enrich communication between Aboriginal and non-Aboriginal practitioners, and improve the quality and relevance of services to Aboriginal children and families. Such applications to service development and their potential for the cross cultural communication of important concepts between Aboriginal and non-Aboriginal society will be explored.

This compares and contrasts what Aboriginal Elders and their communities in Alberta have told us is important with what youth resilience theory has been advancing for many years with a view to enhancing protective factors in day-to-day practice.

Our hope is that by juxtaposing these two perspectives we can begin to develop a common language that resonates with all people in the development of innovative practice models that enhance child and family well-being. The following quotations were gleaned from sharing circles in Aboriginal communities. As outlined in Table One, we have gathered the quotations under a number of themes relevant to both perspectives; the Aboriginal Worldview and the Childhood Resiliency Concepts.

TABLE ONE: A COMPARISON OF KEY ABORIGINAL WORLDVIEWS AND CHILDHOOD RESILIENCY CONCEPTS

Aboriginal Worldview	Childhood Resiliency Concepts
Kinship and connection to each other	Connection to a community
Spirituality and respect for nature	Church and religious connections
Sharing and respect for each other	Contributing to the community/school
Knowledge of history, culture and language	Sense of identity
Development of traditional skills i.e. drumming—dancing	Sense of competence
Shared parenting and community responsibility for children	Healthy parenting

KINSHIP AND CONNECTION TO EACH OTHER VS. CONNECTION TO A COMMUNITY

One of the things I would like to see is a big healing center where everybody can go in anytime and just be there; to have all our culture and language in there. I think what I want is our culture and our language back. We would have our Elders, the youth, children, families to be in there together just to go in and do all kinds of things. I'm thinking about it just getting back to the way I was raised by my grandparents. It is hard to talk about because they are not here anymore. I want to see my grandkids being there with me like I was with my grandparents, because they were really into the culture and my grandmother actually taught me a lot of things. We used to go berry picking, and making dry meat and stuff like that and that is what I would like to see for myself and other families. I want to see the closeness back the way it was, to be a teacher for the young children in the way it was done. One of the main things is learning to respect themselves, respect people, respect the community; all of Mother Earth.

SPIRITUALITY AND RESPECT FOR NATURE VS. CHURCH AND RELIGIOUS CONNECTIONS

I took up believing and trusting in God because I couldn't trust anything else, that's what I had. And he was always there and he never left me. My Creator was there all the time and that's my inspiration. I've learned to forgive and to start trusting. Little children, people, and adults, I try to help them in every way I can today.

This Elder chose me as I was standing there beside the fire. I didn't know what was supposed to be done. Everybody had their own little groups. Everybody knew everybody from the Pow Wow trail or had done the Sweats before so I was by myself. I didn't know what was expected of me. I stood there and this Elder came and talked to me. Apparently we stood there for an hour and a half, it just seemed as though I stood there for fifteen minutes and he started talking to me about the Creator and about the grandfathers and the grandmothers, relatives that had passed on. He explained to me that there is no such thing as hell. He explained to me the four principles of life, the four directions. Anyway he said to me, that old man . . . he's passed on now . . . he said "Who's Jesus?" I could not answer him because I learned all about Jesus through the residential school. Then he said "Jesus was

114

*never here, the man in the black robe . . . he said this in Cree . . .
he brought him over in a big ship". He said "your grandfather and
your grandmother never knew who Jesus was." And that day, that
word stuck in my mind and ever since then, I have followed the
traditional way of life.*

SHARING AND RESPECT FOR EACH OTHER VS. CONTRIBUTING TO THE COMMUNITY/SCHOOL

*I want to be able to see a community that's unified, that can
discuss things together, and that can work together as opposed to
fighting against each other. If we could take our negative energy
and turn it into positive energy the things we can accomplish are
phenomenal . . . but we have to believe in ourselves. I would like
to see people taking responsibility for themselves . . . but a lot of
times we are so busy blaming everybody else [that] we forget to
look at ourselves and [realize] that we have choices. We choose
how we live, if we choose drugs and alcohol then of course the
negativity is going to come with it and we are not going to have
the lives that we want, but if we choose a more positive lifestyle
and take the responsibility for ourselves and say 'yes we were a
part of it and we want to make things happen', then things can
change.*

---

*I would like to see people not being afraid of people. There is [so
much] fear, they are scared to talk to people. The trust is lacking
[and people] are scared to even share their pain. I can remember
people would come to the road and say 'hi, what's your name,
where are you from, come in have coffee, come in rest up' even
[if you were] just walking a little ways. I would like to see that
happen again.*

Dr. Jean Lafrance

KNOWLEDGE OF HISTORY, CULTURE AND LANGUAGE VS. SENSE OF IDENTITY

I went to a couple of culture camps this year and the things that I saw at the culture camp were good. It was almost as if the people acted differently, not like here in everyday life. In the culture camp they were just laughing and having a good time. I don't know if I was the only one guy who saw this, but that would be something I would like to see more of.

Every child should have a Blackfoot name. I think it's very important because that places us in the universe and it places us in connection with all our relatives. It's a powerful strength that we have, to have our Blackfoot names. But it does not have any meaning if you don't know what those connections are or if you don't know how to be in relationship with those connections or with those alliances. An Elder will give a name and so when you get your name, you say "This is who I am and this is the Elder who gave me my name" so there's a connection to an Elder and this is the story of why they gave you that name and a lot is tied to it. This gives us strength as every time you say your name you have all these connections and all these alliances that place you; who you are, where you came from, and where are you going.

We've got our stories but they've been marginalized. One of our students came up with this notion of storycide, you know like genocide; storycide. Our stories are very, very important and again you have to look at the Blackfoot words that capture it. It means a lot more than saying the story (in English) because in that language it's got negative connotations. In English it's just a story but for us, they're not just stories. Those stories contain so much and we need to get back to them. Those stories serve us in so many different ways. How do we remember these stories? [Because] the art of storytelling was so much a part of us. Some of the best storytellers are so animated and a good storyteller has the ability for you to experience the story, to see the story. Our way of learning is to use all the five senses, and that's how they tell the stories. I guess the closest thing to that would be a good novel. If it's really well written, that novel stays with you; for us it's our oral tradition.

DEVELOPMENT OF TRADITIONAL SKILLS VS. SENSE OF COMPETENCE AND SKILL

I went to Onion Lake a little while ago and you should have seen the young people dance around; just the young people, even the little kids were playing drums. That's what they should teach. People here should teach the young people to play drums and dance; all the dances [such as] round dances. When I go to dances here I don't see young people get up to dance.

I think I did a good thing this one weekend. Everyone was having a party after a tournament and I had no booze to buy so I couldn't give a drinking party. These people wanted to go somewhere so I brought them home, no booze no nothing, and they sat around on the floor and on the chairs in my dining room and living room, and I just put a bag of dry meat there and that was our party. The next day they called it our dry meat party. So I feel proud of myself doing that. I didn't have lots of dry meat but I just put it there and they went home about 1:30 and that was that, so I felt good about myself. I don't have lots but I was willing and the next day some people come there to ask for dry meat. They were trying to buy some but I don't sell.

COMMUNITY RESPONSIBILITY FOR CHILDREN VS. HEALTHY PARENTING

I'm granny. Long ago, as far as I know, our people had their way of raising their families. We had the grandparents, we had the aunts and uncles and then we had the parents themselves. Our grandparents were there to teach us. They were our teachers. If we wanted to know something we approached our grandparents and they taught us what they knew and our aunts and uncles were the people that told us when we did something wrong. When we did something wrong it wasn't our parents that scolded us or told us what we did was wrong. It was up to the aunts and uncles. They were the ones that disciplined their nephews and nieces and I still see that sometimes today. Sometimes one of my sons when his nephews do wrong, he tells them they did wrong. He doesn't wait for the parents to tell them. He tells them. That's the way it was long ago and the parents were there just to love their kids. You gave love to your kids and your kids loved you in return. The children didn't have to be taken out of homes and when they were orphaned or the parents were sick, the rest of the family was there to just take them in and look after them. There was no such thing as who is going to take care of this child, somebody just said you can come home and live with me. I'll raise you and take care of you and that was it.

I would say one of the customs was that the oldest would go and live with the grandparents. But other than that, I think now from what I understand, you had a favourite uncle or a favourite aunt who kind of took over and was also almost like another parent so that gave support to the raising of children so people had their favourite nieces or nephews. I know I had a favourite aunt whom I always went to on weekends or during holidays. I think overall the assumption has always been that First Nation or Aboriginal people cannot take care of their children. That we don't have either the capability or the ability and these are basically the two main reasons children are apprehended . . . the unwillingness or inability to take care of children. I think when you look at the policy of colonization, it started off with "Let's remove the children, let's take the children away from their homes because the parents cannot take care of them. We'll Christianize them, we'll civilize them" and I think today, when I say it's a constructed reality, we come from that place. Many institutions that are based on a dominant ideology and social policy come from "we can't take care of our children." We've just perpetuated that initial policy about removing children.

I feel the need to teach the young people today. They don't understand the love that we have for them. I think that they need to know that we love them. Our children have been affected by our not knowing how to show our love for them. They need the hugs and to hear that we love them because we don't know how. As soon as you try to hug somebody well you feel bad. Our parents did not show it to us because they were not there and it makes children think that they are not loved but they are. It is we who don't know how to show it. We need to put that love back. I helped my daughter with a group of people about 3 or 4 days ago and one of my nieces asked me what kind of soup it was and I said love soup. I made it with love. The parents are suffering too because they were raised without the love that they should have had . . . I think sometimes we feel that if we tell our children

119

that they might say well, what are you talking about? You never showed it . . . That's one thing that the convent took away from us. They were never parents and they never gave birth to a kid.

DISCUSSION

The removal of Aboriginal children from home and community has deprived them of a tightly knit community of extended family and relatives who shared the task of childrearing. The separation of children from parents and the loss of parental role models has contributed to many of the child care problems of Aboriginal parents (McKenzie and Hudson 1985). Aboriginal children who spent many years in residential schools had limited experience as family members (Haig-Brown, 1988). Atteneave (1977, p 30) recollects that "Neither they nor their own parents had ever known life in a family from the age they first entered school. The parents had no memories and no patterns to follow in rearing children except for the regimentation of mass sleeping and impersonal schedules." This lack of positive role modeling has taken its toll in the Aboriginal family in Canada today.

Since Aboriginal people attribute many of their losses to colonialism and the oppressive systems that attempted to take away their history, traditions, language, and identity, it should not be surprising that many would seek a return to health and autonomy via their history, a traditional way of life, a rediscovery of language, and a sense of identity as an Aboriginal person. While many Aboriginal child welfare agencies are seeking models of practice that are more consistent with their own worldviews, there is a dearth of models that incorporate "old" ways to respond to our "new" understanding of the impact of residential school experiences and the 60s scoop on Aboriginal communities and families. The challenge is to learn from a dialogue that will not only create new knowledge, but one that can be readily applied to real world situations.

The creation of this vision is not without its challenges. On the one hand, there is a strong and continuing desire among many Aboriginal people and their allies to build upon traditional Aboriginal strengths and values such as courage, respect for each other and for nature, the oral tradition and the wisdom of the Elders, a deep connection with each other and Mother Earth, and a consistent application of spirituality to all of life. On the other hand, the loss of culture and tradition that has resulted from colonization continues to affect the lives of Aboriginal people.

As child welfare services have evolved over the past century, the adoption of a bureaucratic and legalistic paradigm seems to have increasingly rigidified practice by the introduction of overly specialized roles, top down and fiscally driven policies, increasing disconnection from community, overly prescriptive standards, and other trappings of technologically based approaches that create increasing distance between child welfare practitioners and those they serve. Yet these are the models provided to Aboriginal service providers. What we propose is to bring together the best of Indigenous and Western approaches by strengthening elements of interconnectedness and spirituality to child welfare practice in all of our communities. Our destinies are so intertwined; only by bringing together the full force of our understanding can we reverse the actions of past generations and create new approaches based upon lessons critical to our common future. This leaves us with a fundamental question, especially for non-Aboriginal child welfare professionals who are still working closely with Aboriginal children, families and communities. The question is "what can be done about this now?"

REFLECTIONS

1. In light of the lucidity and wisdom of the Aboriginal people who contributed to this chapter, how can there be any doubt that they have the capacity to look after their children in a way that is far superior to anything that is offered to them away from their communities?
2. Why do we have so much ease in the identification of the deficiencies of Aboriginal communities and so much difficulty in recognizing the amazing strengths that have enabled them to survive as a people in spite of so many efforts to decimate them?

SOURCES

It is most important that we recognize the contribution of the Sturgeon Lake First Nation who allowed me to join them in their Journey toward Empowerment where the community came together to reflect upon their current situation. The stories in this chapter were gleaned from the sharing of their stories that have had such a profound impact on my life and that continue to form the foundation for what has become my life mission. The Journey toward Empowerment is available from the author in PDF form by emailing me at Lafrance@ucalgary.ca.

Atteneave, C. (1977). *The Wasted Strengths of Indian Families in the Destruction of American Indian Families.* In Unger, S. (Ed.) New York: Association on American Indian Affairs.

Berry, S., & Brink, J. (2004). *Aboriginal cultures in Alberta: Five hundred generations.* Edmonton, Alberta: The Provincial Museum of Alberta.

Blackstock, C., Trocmé, N., & Bennett, M. (2004). Child welfare response to Aboriginal and non-Aboriginal children in Canada: A comparative analysis. *Violence against women, 10*(8), 901-916.

Dion Stout, M. & Kipling, G. (2003). *Aboriginal People, Resilience and the Residential School Legacy.* The Aboriginal Healing Foundation Research Series.

Haig-Brown, C. (1988). *Resistance and Renewal.* Vancouver: Tillacum Library.

Health Canada. (2000). *Statistical profile on the health of First Nations in Canada.* Retrieved February 19, 2006, from http://www.hc-sc.gc.ca/fnih-spni/pubs/gen/stats_profil_e.html

Hunter, S., & Lewis, P. (2006). *Embedding Culture for a Positive Future for Koori Kids.* Victorian Aboriginal Child Care Agency. Unpublished Presentation. (ACWA Conference).

Laboucane-Benson, P. (2005) A Complex Ecological Framework of Aboriginal Family Resilience. Paper for Edinburgh Conference. Native Counseling Services of Alberta.

Lafrance, J. et al. (2008). Synchronicity or Serendipity? Aboriginal Wisdom and Childhood Resilience in Liebenberg L., & Ungar M., editors, *Resilience in Action*. University of Toronto Press; Toronto, 2008, pp. 289-320.

Lalonde, C. (2006). Identity Formation and Cultural Resilience in Aboriginal Communities. In Flynn, R.J., Dudding, P., & Barber, J. (Eds.) *Promoting Resilient Development in Young People Receiving Care: International Perspectives on Theory, Research, Practice & Policy* (pp. 52-71). Ottawa, ON: University of Ottawa Press.

McKenzie. B. & Hudson, P. (1985). Aboriginal Children, Child welfare, and the Colonization of Aboriginal Children. In K. L. Levitt & B. Wharf (Eds.), *The Challenge of Child welfare* (pp. 125-141). Vancouver, BC: UBC Press.

Chapter 9

Summing It Up:
What Can Be Done About This Now?

This chapter addresses in more concrete terms what Aboriginal people have said is important to them. It includes some ideas about what they can do as a community and what can be done in child welfare practice that will assist them in the achievement of a new vision for their children. The following table describes what we have learned from Aboriginal people and makes suggestions for practice. It includes stories from the heart, academic theories, and historical facts. The most important part of this learning occurs when you can take what you are feeling in your heart, think it through, and put it into practice. This section looks at how you can do this.

Why is it important for you to go through this process, for you to take what is in your heart and make it part of your practice? Because broken children become broken adults; the time for change is now, and the person who can be that change is you.

The following framework was developed by our mostly Aboriginal BSW students at Blue Quills College near St. Paul, Alberta. It is instructive to note that they arose spontaneously at my request during a class on social policy. This confirmed my growing belief that Aboriginal people know exactly what to do to fulfill their vision. All of these students are now working in a wide variety of social work positions within their communities.

PRACTICE SUGGESTIONS
ON IMPORTANT ISSUES

THEME or ISSUE	SUGGESTIONS for PRACTICE
Children need to feel like they belong	Find creative ways to sustain connections with family and community; Work with communities to have Homecoming celebrations for all children in care; Help connect children in care with *at least* one mentor; Foster parents required to connect children in their care with members of the child's community; Find creative ways to ensure that children feel like they belong, that they are unique and special (for example, have groups for kids in care to connect with one another, or a big brother/big sister program for kids in care).
Parents need to be supported and respected	Many parents have been through the residential school or child welfare system themselves, and therefore have a great mistrust of child welfare workers. Take the time to build a relationship with the parents and other involved family members; give them a reason to have confidence in you; Support parents before removing children from home; Work with parents in strategizing and implementing case plans; take the time to hear what the parents need and what they want for their family. Include them in the decision making process; Set up family visits outside of the office setting, and provide families with some privacy and autonomy while they are visiting. Help provide re-parenting support for parents who have not been parented themselves; Educate yourself about the history of the parents. Were they in care? What role models did they have in parenting? Ask them what they need, and support them to get it.

Traditional practices and customs are important	Learn about the traditional ways of the community that you work with. Attend workshops, read books;
	Involve yourself with the community to organize cultural camps once a year for all kids in care;
	Work with community members to create groups for children to experience Aboriginal community life;
	Seek out Elders as mentors;
	Seek out Elders to provide traditional teachings to children in care;
	Seek out Elders to provide traditional teaching to staff working with the children;
	Request the involvement of Elders in case planning and community planning;
	Arrange with the community for a naming ceremony for every child in care;
	Arrange Father and Son; Father and Daughter days;
	Finance transportation to community based events for the off-reserve kids;
	Use Friendship Centers for kids in urban areas—provide them with a space to connect with other kids in care, their family members, and Elders.
Community Capacity Building	Complete a Community inventory; what is in place, what is missing? From here create a Community plan that is *based on the community's needs;* this would need to include all stakeholders (workers, parents, children, Elders);
	Support and seek out Kinship Care alternatives rather than removing kids from their communities;
	Go into the community with questions and an open mind rather than a plan; build relationships, find out what the community needs and what the community has, and work together to find solutions;
	Develop programs that address intergenerational trauma; start with education and awareness, and see where the community needs to go from there.

Prevention instead of Intervention	Establish what the strengths and the needs are in the community; work with the strengths to meet the needs;
	Allow the family to identify their own needs . . . and then help them meet those needs;
	Focus on family wellness; prenatal classes, early education, and family support based on traditional teachings;
	Understand the importance of community, and of collective wellness; individuality and individual healing are Western thoughts, and have no place in Aboriginal communities;
	Instead of taking children from their home, provide in home support and mentorship for families in crisis;
	Implement a program for community crisis support team, a team of community members who are trained in crisis intervention. They stay with the children if parents have to leave, rather than apprehending children in the middle of the night;
	Provide childcare and respite care for single mothers; provide a space where single mothers can gather together and support one another;
	Provide a wellness program for fathers, with Elders as facilitators and mentors for the young men.

Broken children become broken adults; the time
for change is now and the person who can be that
change is you.

POLICY IMPLICATIONS

It seems that by creating such a convergence of our two rivers, Aboriginal and Western, we might be able to create new knowledge that would not only better serve Aboriginal communities, but all communities, while retaining the fundamental integrity of our respective world views. This would require the hard work of sharing our experience and how we are feeling about matters of importance to us and helping the other to understand, then reciprocating this experience. It seems to us that by creating a convergence of our two rivers, Aboriginal and "mainstream", for lack of a more descriptive term, it is possible to create new knowledge that would not only better serve Aboriginal communities, but all communities. To achieve this vision; we need to think about the following possibilities:

- Commit to a concerted effort between provincial authorities and Aboriginal people to ensure that the destructive federal fiscal policy that has been in place for over a century is rescinded and replaced by one that does not result in the continuing removal of children from their families and communities.
- Consider the contribution of Aboriginal spirituality to a holistic and community centered practice model.
- Learn from Aboriginal people's history of oppression and the outcomes that continue to plague them today.
- Learn about Aboriginal world views by connecting and relating with an Aboriginal mentor and guide.
- Be prepared to listen to the perspectives of Aboriginal communities.

There are practical ways of thinking about services that are governed by the learning that has occurred, and we are hopeful that they will improve matters for Aboriginal children, families and communities. We hope that our work will generate increased operational specificity in program development guided by the principles enunciated by our communities, such as the importance of culture, community, kinship, identity, and respect. This will be addressed by continued exploration and study of our history with Aboriginal communities, to learn from past experiences and to correct these for future generations. We will also examine, document and evaluate promising programs and practices that better meet the needs of Aboriginal children and that help to live out the values and principles that communities have taught us.

While each community has to determine its own needs in this search, we present some possibilities for consideration. In the short term, several opportunities present themselves. One legacy of the residential school experience is that Aboriginal children are disproportionately represented even today in foster homes and youth detention facilities. The rebuilding of cultural traditions is a key step to overcoming this problem. This process of rebuilding will require that we make resources available directly to Aboriginal communities so that they can develop language, cultural, spiritual, and educational programs. The Aboriginal Healing Foundation has taken a beginning step in this direction, one that could benefit from appropriate partnerships with university researchers and mainstream service providers who are sensitive to the Aboriginal reality of today.

It is also clear that Aboriginal agencies continue to operate with even more inadequate financial resources than non-Aboriginal agencies. The current funding formula not only restricts Aboriginal agencies from offering preventive programs, it provides limited flexibility to offer innovative programs that are consistent with traditional values and approaches. This could be a priority area for collaboration, with academics and policy makers exercising a concerted effort to educate federal funding sources regarding the potential efficacy of such approaches over the long term. It also seems clear that many Aboriginal agencies are operating in a policy vacuum because they have not had the time to develop policies, standards, and protocols that are responsive to their unique situations. A collaborative effort would have a greater likelihood of success than isolated efforts to promote change. In this process, special attention must be given to the provision of sufficient resources to Aboriginal agencies to address the complex and serious problems that confront them on a daily basis.

In the longer term, and as an overriding principle, we need to begin by recognizing our interdependence with clients, community, and stakeholders. The next section involves a list of Systemic Recommendations which flow from this principle; while they are not exhaustive, they could serve as a starting point. It will be clear to anyone with even a nodding acquaintance with current child welfare practice that these suggestions do not reflect the reality of practice today. In fact, they are often the antithesis of much of current practice. This makes them even more important from a transfer of learning perspective, since much of the research over the past decade has led us in this direction, but core functions in child welfare rarely reflect these new realities.

It is proposed that we can best ensure success by becoming aware of the influence of prevailing paradigms upon our practice. Rappaport (1981) proposes that there is no one best way to solve the problems that face us, but that there are many divergent ways which deserve the joint attention of communities, service providers, and academics.

The difficulty involved with change cannot be underestimated, but each of us can point to examples that illustrate the possibility of achieving a partnership between Aboriginal communities and the mainstream institution of child welfare. It will require that we step out of expected and typical institutional relationships to find a common ground of caring, respect, and flexibility, as well as an orientation toward action from a research and an educational perspective.

The community, policy makers, and the university can work together to incorporate knowledge from "mainstream" theory, practice, and research pertaining to children's services with the traditional wisdom of First Nations communities. This path of mutual respect asks all of us to drop the barriers that keep us apart. It is a path that calls on each of us to reflect upon each other's view of reality, as we find ways to work together to solve problems that would be unmanageable on our own.

Don Juan's advised Carlos Castaneda about taking a path with a heart. Here are his encouraging words for those who fear the unknown,

> *A path without a heart is never enjoyable. You have to work hard even to take it. On the other hand, a path with a heart is easy: it does not make you work hard at liking it.*

We think that this path has a heart.

SYSTEMIC RECOMMENDATIONS

The following are critical if substantive systemic change is to occur:

- We must collectively support a legislative framework that provides a higher degree of self-determination for Aboriginal people who wish to serve their own families and children.

- Program funding must be on a par with any other community in similar social, economic, educational and health circumstances and provide a full range of services needed to address the numerous issues that have evolved over the past 500 hundred years.

- We must understand how traditional ways have sustained Aboriginal families for thousands of years without white intervention, and build upon them to create a new society.

- We must co-create new knowledge in the search for answers that can replace the increasingly complex responses created to serve families and children.

- We must fully implement the Convention on Indigenous People's Rights of 1948 which, if taken seriously, would have made a dramatic in the lives of Aboriginal people over the past half century.

- We must recognize Indigenous people as a people with a living history and with ideas, thought, imaginations, and caring. There is a need to place confidence in them and to assist them where we can in the development of approaches that will better serve their communities and their families.

- We must create a political will at the federal and provincial levels that will sustain and support Aboriginal aspirations and finally remove them from the shackles that are imposed on them. We must release the need for control that is embedded in a collective and fundamental racism that leaves Aboriginal families disrespected and with few reasonable alternatives.

- We must develop approaches that stress interconnectedness, self-determination, and equity with others. All communities stressed the importance of human connection as a fundamental requirement for creating a new vision for the future. All communities stressed the importance of self-determination and freedom to experiment and to do things as they see fit, just like any other community.

- We can no longer tolerate attitudes that constrain equity and fair treatment; we must combat the view that Aboriginal people are somehow less worthy, less intelligent, and less moral as some in our society assumed.

These recommendations demand a major paradigm shift. They call on us to face the most difficult challenge of all, to change our beliefs and our very ways of thinking. This requires commitment, goodwill, mutual respect, and trust. This will not come easily in light of our prior experiences, but it is nevertheless of critical importance.

We began this initiative with the intention of helping to create new models of practice that would recognize the trauma and pain that are the legacy of provincial and federal child welfare systems. Aboriginal people have given us the guideposts upon which to base such an objective. The fundamentals are clearly understood by Aboriginal leaders and Elders. The problem is that the same fundamentals are poorly understood and even less readily accepted by so many others. An important step is to accept the fundamentals, not only at an intellectual level, but at an emotional level, grounded in our common humanity and in our relationships as human beings.

We have experienced great trust on the part of communities to develop new models of practice that are in keeping with tradition and culture. We have every reason to believe that this is an important and achievable objective. The worrisome part is that unless we are grounded in the philosophy and wisdom of the Elders, we could be simply recreating new versions of models that are based on our own false thinking.

Our challenge is not to only create new models, but to change our thinking and our actions. We can only achieve this by respecting and acting upon the advice of the Aboriginal community and its precious Elders. We cannot do less. The following is offered as one way to integrate some of the holistic approaches favored by Aboriginal people in a largely bureaucratic system. We hope you will look at it as one option by which to change practice and/or policy, not only to better integrate these with an Aboriginal worldview, but also with a fundamentally human perspective.

REFLECTIONS

1. Are any of the ideas discussed already put into practice in your organization? If so, how well are they working?
2. In your opinion, are these suggestions realistic? Can you see yourself and your organization implementing some of these ideas into practice?
3. Do you see the value in using some of these ideas in your practice?
4. Who would support you and your organization in implementing these ideas into practice?
5. Who or what would be an obstacle in implementing some of these ideas into practice?
6. What needs to change in your practice and your organization in order for these ideas to be implemented?

PART III

Aboriginal World Views and the Administrative State

THIS SECTION IS DIRECTED TO POLICY
MAKERS, POLITICIANS, PROGRAM PLANNERS,
ADMINISTRATORS AND ALL OF US WHO ARE
RESPONSIBLE FOR THE CREATION OF PROGRAMS
THAT WORK FOR THOSE WE SERVE.

Chapter 10

Aboriginal Worldviews and Child Welfare Reform

Part two provided an overview of four different orientations to program change in child welfare, as told by Aboriginal people and front line workers. Within the context of Aboriginal communities, the complexities of knowledge mobilization are magnified. While Aboriginal people are varied and have distinctive cultures, languages, histories and traditions, it seems clear that Indigenous people from around the world are united in a common vision of serving their people in ways that are true to themselves.

Although there is a need to create new knowledge to fill existing service gaps, it is also clear that there are few described notions of how to achieve this. Aboriginal communities are, however, clear about the essential values and philosophy that must guide the development of programs and services.

In this regard, Little Bear (2000) speaks of the collision of "jagged worldviews," aiding our understanding of the differences between Aboriginal and Eurocentric worldviews. In contrast to First Nations, Eurocentric philosophies are more linear than holistic; hierarchical and specialized rather than generalized; more materialistic and self-interested than sharing; less concerned about relationships and kindness than competitiveness; more aggressive than respectful; and more focussed on external sources of control and authority than on the development of internal controls. The complex historical interaction of these two approaches has left a heritage of jagged worldviews among Indigenous people who no longer have a clear grasp on either worldview. This leads to a jigsaw puzzle type of consciousness that each person has to piece together alone.

MAKING OUR HEARTS SING (MOHS) INITIATIVE

The Making our Hearts Sing Initiative provided many forums within which Aboriginal people could express their vision for a child welfare service that better meets their needs and that is consistent with their world views.

The Making our Hearts Sing (MOHS) gathering was a coming together of the Blood Tribe (Kainai Nation), the Sturgeon Lake Cree Nation and Métis representatives at the Nakoda Lodge west of Calgary. In this deeply spiritual place in the foothills of the Rocky Mountains, and in follow up to the Making our Hearts Sing initiative, about 80 participants from these communities, including Elders, council members, youth, community members and interested professionals came together to share their thoughts on what might be done at a concrete level to achieve their aspirations to create an improved child welfare system that would work best with their communities.

As demonstrated by community members' commentary, the fundamentals are still very much alive in Aboriginal communities. For those who shared their stories, the most meaningful experiences resided in their relationships; some as permanent as that of a grandparent, some as transitory as a chance encounter. All these stories contain a common thread: the importance of being respected and acknowledged by another person. All reflected a sense of being viewed as a person with inherent dignity and worth. All recounted being left with a major impression of being a person with potential and hope for the future because someone believed in them, whether it was a student who was recognized for demonstrating a talent in school, or a new mom whose grandfather show her how to properly care for her new baby. In short, these stories all related fundamentally human experiences that made an important difference in individual lives.

Services need to be structured in ways that reflect the teachings provided by the communities themselves. The following summarizes some key notions that flow from the stories of community members, derived from the MOHS gathering. The intent of this gathering was to invite the participants to reflect upon more concrete ways of addressing the deeply felt solutions that had been expressed in the Making our Hearts Sing initiative. I am grateful to Robin Little Bear, Lance Tailfeathers and their team from the Blood Tribe Legislative Initiative for having led the Open Space process that allowed this rich and diverse set of ideas to emerge. I am also grateful to them and to David Nabew for having organized the Sturgeon Lake contingent for this historic meeting of Blackfoot, Cree and Métis peoples coming together in their common interest for their children.

KEY NOTIONS OF MOHS; WHERE DO WE GO FROM HERE?

The following thematic analysis was prepared by Kristine Morris, a former BSW student from the University of Calgary and presently a child welfare worker with a Mi'Kmaw community in Nova Scotia, sums up their thoughts on where we should go from here. In the first set of interviews, participants spoke about problems they have faced in their lives as a result of their residential school experiences.

EFFECTS OF THE RESIDENTIAL SCHOOL EXPERIENCES

The points brought up in their section reinforce the already well-documented effects on children when they are removed from their homes and their cultures. Here are the main themes brought out in this section:

Loss of Identity

- "I didn't belong anywhere"
- "I felt isolated from both worlds"
- "It was a loss of love, a loss of trust, a loss of culture and a loss of language"

Intergenerational Impact

- "I couldn't say 'I love you' to my kids because it was never said to me"
- "I was never taught to show love, and so I never showed it to my kids"
- "I don't know how to raise a family; I was never shown"

It's still happening in the community

- "That chain [of putting kids in care] has to break; it has to break"
- "We're not God . . . to determine how a child should live"
- "Our kids are still being taken from us; we need to get them back"

Another point that came up frequently in the interviews was that in order to start of the journey of healing, one must first tell one's story. This reinforces how important sharing circles like this one are, giving survivors the opportunity to share their stories, to have their experiences heard and validated by their peers; this is the starting point to their healing journey.

WHAT MADE A DIFFERENCE IN MY LIFE

In the telling of "what made a difference in your life?", the main point that came across was that if there was ONE PERSON who made you feel important, who made you feel loved, this had a positive impact on people's lives. Once again the theme of relationship was paramount. Highlights from this section are:

Elders

- "An Elder taught me the old ways, about the Creator"
- "Elders teach us the way it was; the way it should be"

Parents and Extended Family

- "I was raised by my mom for the first 4 years"

- "My grandfather taught me respect and parenting skills"
- "My grandmother taught me respect, honesty and forgiveness"
- "My grandfather taught me the old ways of hunting and fishing; I was proud of who I was"
- "My sister encouraged me to go to university, and I did it"
- "My father cried when I lost my first child; I didn't know that men cried"
- "My mother told me that I would become something one day, and I believed her"
- "My dad convinced me not to give up my son"
- "My mom fostered kids on the reserve, and she didn't drink"
- "My mom never said that I couldn't be what I wanted to be"

Children

- "I learned to realize that a little child is more important than I am"
- "I realized that I had to protect my child, and so I had to get it together"
- "My child deserved a better life"
- "Children trust you, you can't let them down"
- "My grandchildren inspire me . . . I think I'm their inspiration, too"

The Community

- "I must have got lucky and I had people believe in me, all over the place . . ."

- "Made to feel welcome and accepted when I went home [to the reserve]"
- "This circle"
- "Finding people who were willing to say hello to me, that I was worth saying hello to"
- "It felt like I belonged somewhere [when encouraged to play guitar for the community]"

It is worth noting that the community found much of their inspiration in the children; many expressed that the children's presence, their need for parenting, encouraged people to 'do better', to 'try harder'. Children give hope to a community, and the community will work to provide for its children. If this is the case, what happens when there are no children there to work for, no children there to give you hope?

WHAT IS NEEDED TO MAKE A DIFFERENCE IN THE COMMUNITY?

The next section focuses on ideas from the group regarding what is needed to make a difference in the community. The themes in this section were clearly, repeatedly and emphatically expressed by the participants.

Keeping Children at Home

- "Open your eyes, your heart, your soul, and take care of our kids"
- "Stop the cycle [of separating children from families]"
- "I want to see children here at the res; to grow up on the res"
- "Kids need to be in the community"

- "Kids, they're wandering souls out there; they need to be home"
- "Our community needs to be able to see our kids, or better yet to have our kids right here"
- "Keep the kids who are in care connected with their community"
- "I would like to see the community involved when our children are in care, for there to be one person to visit them so they don't feel abandoned"
- "Elders should be involved with the kids that are in care"

Working with the Family System

- "The whole family needs to be worked with"
- "Rather than removing kids, work with the whole family"
- "If the problem is with the parents, the parents should be the ones put in a different place, not the children . . . it's not the children's fault"
- "In the first 5-6 years, they only need one consistent adult. They'll be able to handle anything later on . . . just give them a parent, a grandparent who will be there for them everyday"
- "Parents need to be there in the morning and when they come home from school"
- "I try to show my daughter how to love her kids"
- "It's up to us to show the younger people, the next generation how to do things"
- "It's about the families; it's about teaching values and, you know, even having supper together"
- "We need to support the families in each community"

- "Elders could be used to mediate between children's services and families"
- "Involve Elders in child custody decisions; they know the family, they know the community"
- "The whole community needs to spend time with the children"
- ". . . need parents, grandparents to get involved"
- "We all need to take time for the kids"

Reclaiming (and Teaching) Indigenous Ways of Knowing

- "Use spirituality, Elders and traditional teachings to heal our kids"
- "Offer a traditional camp for our young people"
- "We've tried to adopt too much of the white man's way . . . we're not holistic anymore"
- "We have to teach our white brothers who we are, whether they like it or not, because they are making the policies and they are looking after some of our kids"
- "Teach policy makers to see things from an Aboriginal perspective"
- "Teach social work students more about colonization, oppression, and diversity"

Include Children in the Solution

- "Push policy makers to include kids' needs into policy making"
- "Children need to be included in the conversation"
- "There is an empty seat here—where are the children, in this conversation about their future?"

The Devolution of Child welfare

- "Child welfare needs to devolve and take a holistic approach"
- "We need proper funding for programs"
- "A better distribution of funds, to be statistically on par with other Albertans"
- "Coordinate existing resources on the reserve; the friendship center, in-home liaison people, education, social work, and Elders"
- "Child welfare has to realize that every child is special"
- "Aboriginal foster homes are needed"
- "Aboriginal social workers"
- "Child welfare needs to remember that it's a very lonely world out there when you're little, you're alone and you're waiting to come home"

In reviewing the themes from this set of interviews, it is obvious that this group of participants is very clear on what is needed in the community. The overwhelming response is that families need to be kept together, that they need the supports for this to happen, and that policy makers need to hear this demand. The challenge now is to channel these strongly felt aspirations and use them as the foundation in forming a new way of practicing child welfare. While the aspirations and ideas are present, there still seems to be a considerable distance to travel before this vision can be achieved. It seems that hopes are too often thwarted by the very systems that have been established to assist Aboriginal children, families, and communities. The question of how to get past these barriers is then posed to those who create the very obstacles to the fulfillment of that vision—the administrative and legal state.

REFLECTIONS

1. How do the values of First Nations communities mesh or conflict with those of government organizations that are based on a bureaucratic model?
2. What are the trade-offs between considerations of efficiency vis-à-vis those of effectiveness?
3. How do we reconcile the values of a hierarchical, specialized, and highly structured system with one that tends to be collegial, generalized and flexible?
4. Is it not possible to develop an array of voluntary programs that are culturally relevant and that fulfill the same needs that are met in our towns and cities for the general population?
5. Could we not strengthen and support the capacity building efforts of Aboriginal communities?
6. Could we not learn from Aboriginal communities how to minimize the negative aspects of bureaucratic systems and enhance the human and spiritual to the betterment of all of our helping systems?

SOURCES

The eighty participants from the Blood Tribe, the Sturgeon Lake Cree Nation and Métis communities, including Elders, community leaders, families and youth. Their hard work over a two day period in an open space forum facilitated by Blood Tribe staff produced 600 written recommendations to improve child welfare in their community.

Dr. Jean Lafrance

I am grateful to Robin Little Bear, Lance Tailfeathers and their staff for leading the open space process and to David Nabew for coordinating the Sturgeon Lake contingent.

Finally to my daughter Kristine Morris, who is now a child welfare worker with Mi' Kmaw Family and Children's Services in Nova Scotia for having completed the thematic analysis—thank you!

Chapter 11

Competing Systems and Reconciling The Two: What Do We Need From Each Other?

A SOCIETAL CONUNDRUM

John Ralston Saul, when he wrote "Voltaire's Bastards", described how over many years, the common people had given over the authority to their kings as being in the best position to make decisions or judgments on their behalf. This worked more or less well for many years, until the French Revolution decided that the people no longer wanted a royalty that showed no concern for the people who were starving in the streets.

Ralston Saul speaks of a way of thinking that assumed that such power to care for us could be placed in the hands of those we might call technocrats; highly educated individuals who were prepared to assume leadership roles in considering social issues and developing solutions based on their superior knowledge and competence. This then, would be the basis for our safety; our trust in the intelligence and goodwill of others. In some aspects, this resulted in positive outcomes, and in many western countries became the foundation of fundamental social systems for the old, the poor, the creation of healthcare systems that would protect everyone, for educational systems that would serve all children. Yet even then, some worried about this assumption. Eduard Lindeman spoke eloquently at the beginning of the 20th century about

> *. . . Technologists and specialists insulating themselves from the folk process and becoming each in his own limited sphere, wise in particulars and ignorant in general (Lindeman, 1932).*

Many suspect that the very institutions that have been created to serve our people are far removed from understanding the needs of the people being served. One does not have to reach very far to find examples of how our health, education, legal, and social institutions are failing Aboriginal people. Notably, this includes the one institution that is mandated to serve them, the Department of Northern and Indian Affairs, whose sole reason for being is the existence of Aboriginal people. This system spends billions of dollars annually, much of which never reaches the individual families and communities that continue to live in situations parallel to those of a developing country.

Two theoretical frameworks appeared to hold explanatory potential in this examination: Warren's seminal work on vertical and horizontal systems (1978); and Kweit and Kweit's theories on the premises of bureaucratic decision making (1980). In this instance, vertical systems are those that mainly reside in large

> *The very institutions that have been created to serve our people are far removed from understanding the needs of the people being served.*

governmental institutions such as INAC and the Ministry of Child and Youth Services; while horizontal systems approximate what exists at the Band or community level for Aboriginal people. A powerful metaphor for the dynamics that exist for individuals who must function across both systems is found in the film "Dances with Wolves" where Kevin Costner adopts the lifestyle of the Lakota tribe (horizontal system) only to be severely punished by his military colleagues (vertical system) upon their return.

VERTICAL AND HORIZONTAL SYSTEMS

The discussion begins with an examination of Warren's (1978) work on vertical and horizontal systems. This work is at the heart of understanding the roles of professionals who interact with both vertical and horizontal systems, and the tensions that arise due to the often conflicting expectations of each. Mid-level administrators employed in large human service organizations function at the nexus of vertical and horizontal systems (Warren, 1978). The local administrator of a state operated program, for example, is located at the intersection of the headquarters of the state operation (vertical system), and the local communities being served (horizontal system). The horizontal systems of society are characterized by locality relevant functions, often occurring in primary groups and providing more opportunities for face to face activities which are sources of social support and social participation (Warren, 1978; Litwak, 1970; Berger & Neuhaus, 1984). The vertical systems of the community are those relationships whereby local units are organized and linked to larger systems, whereas horizontal systems are those relationships that local units share with each other.

The values, goals, and behaviors of horizontal and vertical systems do not always coincide, creating difficult situations for those who work at this juncture of society (Warren, 1978). How individual administrators handle the conflicts that can arise in these situations will determine how they are viewed by their superiors. If the horizontal system (the community) even appears to be favored at the expense of the vertical system (the hierarchical organization), an administrator's influence and status may be compromised.

Vertical systems are likely to be characterized as bureaucratic in nature. Bureaucracies possess the following characteristics:

(1) Economy and efficiency,
(2) Stability and permanence,
(3) Role security,
(4) Relative job security,
(5) Impersonality of policies (Stein, 1960).

Horizontal systems are more likely to be characterized as sharing the traits of primary groups, that is, "any small face to face group that stresses positive affect, non-instrumental permanent and diffuse relations, such as family or friend" (Litwak, 1970: 97).

VERTICAL SYSTEMS

A vertical orientation became increasingly prevalent in modern societies as industrialization and urban growth became dominant. Prior to the 1950s, most decision making in America had been focused at the county level. By the 1950s, decisions regarding many local matters were increasingly being influenced or even usurped by departments and/or organizations at the state and federal levels. This was part of a societal trend which resulted in local communities losing their autonomy. They were increasingly influenced by the prevailing mores, values, and socioeconomic forces of the culture at large and by outside policy actions (Martinez Brawley, 1990). As increased levels of funding were provided by federal and state governments, the autonomy of local levels of government continued to be eroded. Service policies, procedures and standards that had been formulated far from the influence of local citizenry began to shape the nature of human services. In turn, this process began to shape and increase the power of administrators who represented funding sources and had the support of state and federal agencies.

Managers of vertically funded and controlled social service systems, who must balance the legitimate demands of their organization's administration with contradictory demands from their communities, are likely to encounter unique challenges. According to Blau's Exchange Theory, (1964) an examination of reciprocal exchanges between social service agencies and the communities they serve can assume that the participants in such arrangements are basically self-interested. Participatory arrangements between formal organizations and communities can provide each with benefits. Participation can provide community members with benefits such as information, prestige, and access to decision making. The agency can benefit from such advantages as political support, advice, information, and voluntary assistance with carrying out the work of the agency. It is assumed that bureaucratic interaction with local communities will be influenced by such considerations.

THE IRON CAGE

Weber wrote of the evolution of an iron cage, a technically ordered, rigid, dehumanized society. Weber had a foreboding of an "iron cage" of bureaucracy and rationality, but he recognized that human beings are not mere subjects molded by socio-cultural forces. We are both creatures and creators of socio-cultural systems. Moreover, even in a socio-cultural system that increasingly institutionalizes and rewards goal oriented rational behavior in pursuit of wealth and material symbols of status, there are other possibilities.

> *No one knows who will live in this cage in the future, or whether at the end of this tremendous development entirely new prophets will arise, or there will be a great rebirth of old ideas and ideals or, if neither, mechanized metrification embellished with a sort of convulsive self-importance. For of the last stage of this cultural development, it might well be truly said: 'Specialists without spirit, sensualists without heart; this nullity imagines that it has obtained a level of civilization never before achieved (Elwell, Retrieved July 27, 2006).*

Even early social workers were becoming concerned about the trend that was taking place, as the organizational machine became even more prevalent in the provision of social services.

> *Philanthropy is becoming a business and a profession, and social agencies have begun to shut away the layman from any active connection with their*

> *function, crushing him beneath a magnificent and*
> *thoroughly perfected machine (Winslow, 1915).*

> *Humanity is acquiring all the right technology for*
> *all the wrong reasons. (Buckminster Fuller).*

In other words, the very institutions that have been created to solve social problems may at times become the greatest obstacle to their resolution. This is not to blame the many dedicated public servants who labor valiantly to promote system change. It is, however, the nature of large bureaucracies. As suggested earlier in the competing drivers of change, the only way that this can be countered is by leveling the playing field so that communities and families have greater influence on the processes at play.

PREMISES OF BUREAUCRATIC DECISION MAKING

It is also expected that bureaucrats will act in accordance with certain basic premises of decision-making. Simon (1976) has argued that bureaucrats bring to bear multiple premises when making decisions. Kweit and Kweit (1980) have adapted this notion and developed a set of premises that help to explain how some administrators might view aspects of citizen participation. The perspectives of bureaucrats toward various types of citizen participation may be influenced by fundamental premises of bureaucratic decision making. Simon (1976) has developed the concept of decision premises, wherein he argues that bureaucrats bring multiple decision premises to any decision circumstance. Kweit and Kweit (1980) have adapted this concept and suggest that these premises determine many of the actions taken by bureaucrats. They are largely unconscious, and can lead to misunderstandings and confusion when bureaucrats and citizens interact.

They propose **four premises of bureaucratic decision making** that may strongly shape managers' perspectives toward citizen participation. These are:

(1) Requirements for expertise,
(2) Regularity and routinization,
(3) Efficiency,
(4) The self-maintenance of the organization.

In the following discussion, these premises will be considered in terms of how they might influence the perspectives of administrators toward citizen participation.

The premise of bureaucratic expertise often leads bureaucrats to overlook or even avoid viewing citizens as experts. Accepting guidance from citizens could endanger a bureaucrat's self-image as an expert. Professionals who have learned to see themselves as experts can feel threatened when their effectiveness is evaluated by those they serve. They can also feel threatened when they are unable to communicate with the community residents they are trying to help (Hodgson, 1984). Following this line of reasoning, if citizens came to be recognized as having expertise, bureaucrats might become more tolerant of citizen participation because their shared expertise could create a common bond. Citizens would then have resources that could affect the nature of their interaction with bureaucrats (Kweit & Kweit, 1981).

The requirement for regularity and routinization in bureaucracies can be a double-edged sword. Because an organization's behavior will be more predictable, citizens may actually find it easier to gain access to decision makers. It may also, however, make the possibility of changes desired by citizens more difficult because the system will be more rigid and therefore less responsive. This seeming paradox can be explained as follows: if an organization is very structured with clearly articulated and specialized sets of roles and functions, it will be easier for outsiders to identify the key decision makers in particular areas. On the other hand, while it may be easier to establish contact with the right individual, the very rigidity that facilitated the contact could make the system less flexible in its response to the changes proposed. Since citizens seeking decision makers usually want some kind of change, the presence of such rigidity will often lead to conflict.

Efficiency is regarded as the single most important characteristic of bureaucracy. On the face of it, citizen and community interaction impedes efficiency, since consultation or dialogue with "less knowledgeable" persons takes time. Assuming that community participants must be "educated" regarding the organizational conception of a problem or an issue, then this very process can alter the usual routine, slow down decision making, and lead to confusion and inefficiency (Kweit & Kweit, 1981).

A final premise of bureaucratic decision making is that of self-maintenance. James Q. Wilson (1973: 9-10) reflects on this premise when he proposes that:

> . . . *The behavior of persons who lead or speak for an organization can best be understood in terms of their efforts to maintain and enhance the organization and their position in it . . . Whatever else organizations seek, they seek to survive.*

Notwithstanding their tendency to establish standard routines, organizations must be flexible enough to adapt to the environment in order to maintain themselves. The implication for citizen participation is that while it may be a destabilizing force, it may also be a useful resource with which to deal with other elements in the environment, becoming a welcome source of support.

It is proposed that the more closely citizens or community groups conform to and appreciate the premises of bureaucratic decision-making, the greater the likelihood of bureaucratic tolerance or even acceptance of citizen participation. Conversely, decreased citizen conformity or disagreement with the premises of bureaucratic decision-making can be expected to decrease bureaucrats' tolerance toward citizen participation.

This raises several questions:

~ Would administrators value experiences with citizens if they believed that the citizens possessed needed expertise?

~ Would experiences with citizens that adhered to the routine and procedures of the bureaucracy be more welcomed by administrators than those that did not conform to such processes?

~ Would participatory arrangements that appeared supportive of the organization be more valued than those that were not supportive or even confrontational?

These questions form one basis for determining how administrators viewed their experiences with citizens in the course of their careers. It is suggested that if the position of

Kweit and Kweit (1981) is valid, the responses to these questions will be in the affirmative.

From the perspective of organizational theory, the organization-community boundary blurs at the point when citizens become involved with an agency in the delivery of services. All organizations try to isolate their core functions from outside influences. It is assumed that not protecting such activities from outside events makes production efficiency difficult to achieve (Clary, 1985; Thompson, 1967). When citizens become involved in the production of agency services, an inherently disruptive ingredient has been introduced within the organizational framework. Since the involvement of citizens as volunteers is not the norm in large public agencies, these types of organizations are not generally prepared nor structured to deal with such a situation.

Warren (1963) contends that the vertical ties within organizations are stronger than the horizontal ties among different units in a community. An important characteristic of the vertical pattern is the:

> . . . Rational, planned, bureaucratically structured
> nature of its ties . . . that are clearly defined through
> contract, charter, legislation or administrative
> promulgation. (p. 242)

The relationship of local offices to their vertical systems is usually prescribed by the objectives and procedures of that system. Large state or provincial departments make strong demands for allegiance upon locally based administrators. These systems provide an important reference group for administrators. In some instances, district administrators are only in a community as transients, and the norms, goals, values and sanctions of their organization become a more pervasive element in their lives than the success of communities in which they work and live.

Social service organizations sometimes provide broad and abstract goal statements to encourage staff interaction with local citizen groups. Such citizen groups, however, may adhere to norms and values that lead them to contradict the views of the organization. Encouragement solely at the ideological level can create confusion and even resistance among staff unless it is accompanied by concrete instructions and a clear sense of the seriousness of the organization's intent (Warren, 1968). Hasenfeld (1980) stresses the importance of such concrete indicators. He asserts that when planned change is laden with ideologies, as is often the case with citizen participation efforts, it usually fails to provide specific and clear guidelines for action. This permits members of the organization to maintain familiar procedures, rather than leading to concrete changes in techniques and new procedures. It appears reasonable to assume that unless ideology is accompanied by the technology required; namely, expertise, role clarity for new tasks and resources, staff will not willingly engage with citizens.

Vertical orientations are task focused and do not usually emphasize relating to units in the horizontal system. Most often, calls for citizen involvement result in public relations exercises so that organizational tasks can be performed with minimal interference. This might lead experienced agency staff to seek concrete signs of commitment from their hierarchies before meaningfully engaging with citizens (Warren, 1968). What some might perceive as staff resistance to periodic organizational edicts for greater citizen participation may in fact be a realistic response on their part. In other words, does the top level leadership actually mean what it is proclaiming?

Technical rationality, with its emphasis on specialization and expertise, pressures to respond to organizational rules, and centralization of authority within the hierarchy, has been the prevailing value in formal organizations (Denhart, 1981). The introduction of new types of members may require that the service system itself be re-conceptualized. One way a bureaucratic organization can cope with the resulting disruption is to differentiate its basic elements in such a way that a better match occurs between what it does and the external demands for action (Lawrence & Lorsch, 1969). Dominant theories conceptualize organizations in terms of one hierarchical structure, dealing with only one type of participant with whom only one form of relationship can be established.

It is important for organizations to recognize that the new structures developed should be congruent with the new tasks that evolve. If these tasks are highly complex and varied, staff cannot function adequately if they are overly structured (Hasenfeld, 1980). It may be necessary to pattern their behavior in a minimal way that allows them considerable initiative (Warren, 1968). Organizations that experienced considerable hostility from their communities over the past decades may have to allow even greater flexibility and latitude at the local level in order to rebuild lost support. If some programs, as has been suggested (Gardner, 1984; Kammerman & Kahn, 1989), must reach out for new alliances and support from their communities, their staff may require greater flexibility in their interactions, even if this is accompanied by increased risks to the organization.

BUREAUCRATIC ORGANIZATIONS: HELP OR HINDRANCE?

Part of the reason for continuing problems may rest in the very institutions that have been created to help Aboriginal children and their families. Over 40 years ago Cohen (1960) pointed out that one of the greatest changes in human services within recent years has been an increase in formal organizational structures with the accompanying paraphernalia of professionalism, regulations and bureaucracy. William James is cited by Cohen (1960) as having foreseen some of the dangers that accompanied the creation of formal organizations when he stated that:

> *Most human institutions, by the purely technical and professional manner in which they come to be administered, end by becoming obstacles to the very purposes which their founders had in view. Notoriously the greatest reforms in many at least of the professions and institutions have been first advocated, or at least have been greatly aided, by laymen rather than by the official keepers of the seal. And there is reason arising from the very nature of a professional and technical institution why it should easily get out of touch with human life. For the scientific and the technical are necessarily the objective, the impersonal, and the intellectual, as distinguished from the subjective, the personal, the individual, and the emotional (p. 34).*

> *One of the greatest changes in human services
> within recent years has been an increase in formal
> organizational structures with the accompanying
> paraphernalia of professionalism, regulations and
> bureaucracy.*

In short, we may, in the immortal words of Pogo, have met the enemy and he is us. Many would agree that social services in general, and child welfare in particular, have fulfilled James' prediction. Child welfare agencies deal with some of the most intimate aspects of the lives of citizens, namely the relationships which exist in families as well as between families and communities. Yet, the bulk of their service modalities are based on technical and professional considerations.

Sieder (1960) contends that a community is characterized by the quality and scope of its educational, health and welfare institutions. When these are used and supported by citizens, then democratic society is in good health. She cautions that when responsibility for the institutional life of the community is relegated entirely to employed officials, whether in the public or private sector, a precious part of our heritage is lost and services fail to achieve their full potential.

It may be worth reflecting on the extent to which our cherished institutions may actually be part of the problem, and that to some extent they have played a role in diminishing the relational aspects of community.

AT THE NEXUS: BETWEEN VERTICAL
AND HORIZONTAL SYSTEMS

APPLICABILITY OF OPEN SYSTEMS THEORY TO
CHILD WELFARE

Wamsley & Zald (1973) remind us that it is in the environment of organizations that we find the major sources of change, especially in public agencies. If one assumes that the community environment plays a major role in the changes that lead public organizations into controversy, it is important to examine how open systems theory can improve our understanding of the interaction between organizations and their communities. This is particularly important because of the turbulent environment which surrounds child welfare organizations today.

Selznick (1957) states that in the study of organizations there is a need to see the enterprise as a whole and to see how it is transformed as new ways of dealing with a changing environment evolve. The leader's job is to test the environment to find out which demands can become real threats, to change the environment by finding allies and other sources of external support, and to arm the organization by creating ways to withstand attacks. We have seen that the child welfare system is in need of allies and supports, not only to preserve itself from attack, but in order to garner the public support necessary to assist families (Gardner, 1984).

Since the 1980s, child welfare agencies have found themselves increasingly isolated from sources of community support and their credibility has been questioned. Many turned inward as a result and have developed more technocratic ways of improving their accountability, a solution that has not succeeded in generating greater community support (Gardner, 1984; Kammerman & Kahn, 1989; Weinbach, 1990).

Barnard (1938) may assist in understanding how child welfare agencies came to be so isolated. He indicates that organizational purpose has no meaning except in an environment, that it can only be defined within the context of its environment. A very general purpose assumes a very general, undifferentiated environment. But when formed more specifically, purpose serves to reduce the environment more definitely, and this then has the effect of changing the purpose to a more specific one. The back and forth of purpose and environment, according to Simon (1976), reacts in successive steps through successive decisions in greater and greater detail.

THE CHANGING PURPOSE OF CHILD WELFARE

Child welfare has alternated its purpose since the early 1980s; it has at times expanded its mandate to be more inclusive of many family needs, and at others has reduced its mandate to that of protecting and serving only those families deemed to be the most serious cases (Kammerman & Kahn, 1989). As they narrowed their mandate, many child welfare jurisdictions assumed that the community would move in to serve those who were no longer eligible for the more narrowly defined services. There is little evidence of a dialogue with communities about this changed mandate that had taken place, nor were provisions put in place to support families now excluded from service.

Kammerman & Kahn (1989) have asked civic leaders and child welfare officials to consider on an urgent basis the need to "talk regularly, directly and frankly to the public" (p. xii) about the problems being faced by families and the social service requirements to meet these needs. It would seem patently clear that a dialectic regarding the more narrowly defined mandates of public child welfare systems must be undertaken, including consideration of the changes which have already taken place over the past decade. As this dialogue takes place, the interdependence of the child welfare system with its environment may become clearer and lead to more appropriate roles and functions.[3]

Rappaport (1981) suggests that the obsession of social work with transforming social studies into something that resembles the natural sciences obscures, distorts and suppresses the legitimacy of issues vital for theorizing about political and social life. His message for the social sciences is that the distance created by an overemphasis on professionalization and specialization detracts from the conversations which should take place between citizens and persons responsible for social programs. This distance decreases the possibility of addressing the practical problems encountered by recipients of service and community members.

A greater dialogue is proposed between government and Aboriginal communities. Do we believe in the need for such activities? If so, do we possess the necessary organizational support, the required skills, or the time necessary to engage in such activities with their communities?

---

[3]   The usage of the terms dialectic and dialogue in this study is with the meaning provided by Webster's Seventh New Collegiate Dictionary. It defines dialectic as a discussion and reasoning by dialogue as a method of intellectual investigation. Dialogue is defined more simply as an exchange of ideas and opinions.

> An overemphasis on professionalization and specialization detracts from the conversations... between citizens and persons responsible for social programs.

Prevailing scientific and philosophical paradigms led society to increasingly seek mechanistic and technical solutions that were derived from the bureaucratic paradigms. As societal problems became increasingly complex and reached proportions never encountered or even imagined before the advent of the Great Depression, those charged with responsibility for solving these problems reached for solutions offered by the prevailing models. This led to large scale program solutions whose hallmarks were efficiency and effectiveness.

While these approaches were deemed necessary and valuable to society, unanticipated problems accompanied their implementation. As programs increasingly relied upon technical expertise, professionalization and specialization to resolve the problems of society, the voices of citizens and recipients of services began to receive less consideration. Some periodically expressed the concern that too great a reliance upon professional/technical approaches left out critical factors, namely, the views and support of the citizens they were intended to serve. For the most part, however, these concerns were ignored.

As time went by, it was recognized in some scientific and philosophical circles that too great a reliance on the technical and professional left many problems unresolved. The positivist model of science became increasingly challenged and even natural scientists began to question the foundations and assumptions of their methods.

Attempts were made over the years to increase citizen involvement in the planning and delivering of social programs. The experience gained from such attempts suggests that the attitudes of those who administer programs are key elements in attaining successful citizen involvement.

The Balance Theory of Coordination (Litwak, 1966) differentiates between primary groups and bureaucracies in society. Primary groups are small face-to-face groups that stress positive affect, non-instrumental permanent and diffuse relations, such as extended family or friends who relate on the basis of intimacy and personal loyalty. Bureaucracies are characterized by economy and efficiency, stability and permanency, and the impersonality of policies (Litwak, 1970). This theoretical formulation suggests that administrators will be more responsive to citizen advice in the value laden areas that characterize primary groups rather than in the technical areas.

It also suggests that administrators' perspectives on citizen participation will be influenced by the resources in their environment. Citizens and community groups may at times possess resources needed by the agency and be seen as forces to be reckoned with. At other times, the agency may find the environment stable enough and consider that it has sufficient resources to maintain itself with less support from the environment.

Weinbach (1990) suggests that the more hostile the external environment, the more rigid will be the bureaucratic procedures generated to respond to these pressures. Conversely, the more supportive the environment, the less the perceived need for bureaucratic forms of accountability solely to protect the organization. This suggests that administrators' perspectives toward community involvements are influenced by the degree of hostility exhibited toward their programs. This theory appears to be validated by recent events in child welfare, which has received considerable public criticism during the past few decades (Kammerman & Kahn, 1989; Besharov, 1975; Rappaport, 1981). This has been accompanied by increased demands for accountability systems which in turn contribute to increased attention to internal reporting systems (Kammerman & Kahn, 1989). It is suggested that this internal focus has detracted from building relationships with community systems that are important to agencies.

How administrators believe they are viewed by their communities is an important question; one that is expected to be a significant factor in each administrator's determination of future directions for citizen participation. The other side of this equation, however, is the attitude of the bureaucrats themselves toward citizen involvements. McNair (1983) has described bureaucrats and citizens as "foul weather friends," and suggests that bureaucrats will only reach out for assistance from citizens when they need their resources. Bureaucrats who perceive their organization to be experiencing difficulties that could benefit from citizen assistance would, according to this theory, be receptive to citizen participation. This suggests an inverse relationship between bureaucratic power and citizen participation. When organizational power is low and citizen resources are high, bureaucrats are more likely to risk closer alliances with citizens to gain a stronger constituency. When organizational power is high, bureaucrats can implement their plans without assistance. One might then expect them to favor organizational stability without the efforts and risks that citizen participation entails.

Given the troubled condition of many social welfare programs today, one could expect many to seriously consider the need for new allies and constituencies (Gardner, 1984). It is suggested that, given the fiscal restraints in the funding of child welfare programs over the past decades, and the increased criticism that has been experienced, many social service administrators may welcome the prospect of greater citizen involvement in their activities.

The implications of these theoretical constructs for child welfare today are inescapable. Our efforts over the past two decades seem to have increased the hostility and suspicion of the public, engendered fear in many of those we serve, created a loss of confidence in our political leaders, and generated a sense of futility and frustration on the part of many staff.

In many ways, the problems experienced by mainstream child welfare systems seem to be fewer in our Aboriginal agencies, both in delegated agencies such as DFNA's as well as in such urban agencies as the Bent Arrow Traditional Healing Society, which offers 17 creative and community based services that engender trust and support at the community level. What can we learn from this?

HORIZONTAL SYSTEMS

To this point the discussion has revolved around the existing vertical systems which are bureaucratic in nature. It is clear that while this type of system is beneficial in certain settings, human services, specifically child welfare, is not one of them. Many agencies working with children, youth, and families have spent considerable time and resources in the development of holistic programs that focus on wellness and connection with family. The implementation of these programs, however, somehow ends up with much the same results as always, getting lost in the bureaucratic policies and procedures that dominate child welfare services. Funders and government provide these agencies with rigid program logic models and evaluation checklists that must be utilized in order to receive funding, and somewhere along the way the programs based on heart and soul—on relationships—lose meaning in translation.

This being the argument, then what is the solution? One cannot simply dissect an existing paradigm or system, pronounce it ineffective and then walk away. In order for meaningful change to occur, then meaningful alternatives must be considered. I would like to present such an alternative: it's called the Relational Chain.

THE RELATIONAL CHAIN

The Relational Chain, a program planning and evaluation model, was developed as a collaboration between myself and Kristine Morris in 2008. Our initial intention in this research was to revisit the traditional program logic model and remodel it in such a way that it would better reflect the relational needs of clients and workers. What we found, however, was that the model itself was a barrier; it was preventing us from taking the leap from relationship based ideas into programs and evaluations that would support these ideas. As we delved deeper into our research, we examined more closely the connections between traditional logic models and the highly bureaucratic system of child welfare; we then reflected on how this is influencing the child welfare system, from programming and evaluation to front line work.

The Relational Chain enhances the program logic model by redirecting the foundation of the model into a horizontal system rather than a vertical one. It addresses issues from the social work lens of people in the context of their environment, with a specific focus on relationships. It acknowledges the connection between individuals, groups, and systems, and their interplay with each other. It promises a refreshing approach to service planning and evaluation that is consistent with a world view that sees everything in the universe as intimately connected; a worldview that quantum physics now reinforces. Following an extended period where the importance of relationship and reflective practice has been diminished, it promises to support a burgeoning of renaissance in relationship based practice, which is a keystone social work value.

PRESENT DAY CHILD WELFARE ORGANIZATIONS

In spite of massive investments of resources, few are satisfied with the outcomes achieved by child welfare services. The current model of practice, based on a vertical, bureaucratic system, is not meeting the needs of Aboriginal children; this has already been discussed at length. In considering this model of practice, a visual may be of assistance:

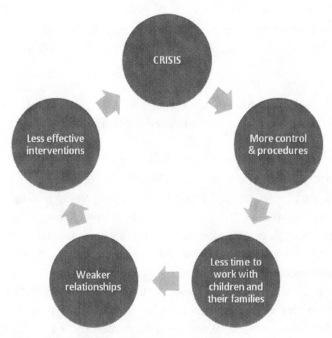

Current model of practice (diagram 1)

As problems continue to arise, the system continues to respond with more rigid, standardized and measurable processes. Changes and revisions seem to be more concerned with achieving the institutional role of gatekeepers to scarce resources and to protect from future litigation than guaranteeing quality children's services. This seems to validate Weber's fear that growing areas of life would be subjected to decision making according to technical rules, diminishing creative thinking and self-direction on the part of its members. He worried that routine and hierarchical decision making might eventually replace discretion, spontaneity, and personal moral choice. Even the casual observer can see that some of these fears have become reality in our child welfare systems. And it is evident in our lost children, broken families, and burned out workers.

THE RENAISSANCE OF RELATIONSHIP BASED CHILD WELFARE PRACTICE

There is a burgeoning interest in the importance of relationship and connection to each other. This interest seems to be driven in part by fatigue and frustration with the rigidly managed, risk-aversive, reactive practices that have invaded social work practice. Ruch (2005) writes of two key characteristics that challenge relationship based practice. First of all, there is the bureaucratic system which, as previously discussed, limits creativity and controls practice with it highly procedural expectations. The other is the reductionist approach to individuals; child welfare organizations implement interventions based on surface problems rather than addressing the root causes. As a consequence, the worker-client relationship focuses primarily on legal and administrative requirements and their associated tasks and outcomes rather than on professional relationships and the complex, relational aspects of the issues. These factors contribute to diminishing the potential for creativity at a time when it is most needed; focusing on rigid policies, procedures and gate keeping rather than on understanding the children and families involved means that the all-important relationships suffer (Houston & Griffiths, p. 2000).

The Relational Chain has been developed in response to this need for the planning and evaluation of relationship based practice. It provides an instrument which has the potential to measure the essence of relationships in human services. And it may help to redress the balance necessary between rationality and relationality.

OBJECTIVES OF THE RELATIONAL CHAIN

Our objective is to assist families in framing their intentions and needs while assisting organizations in creating programs and evaluations that are more fully responsive to the rational *and* relational needs of the most vulnerable of our citizens and those who serve them.

The Relational Chain can be a powerful tool. It can serve to;

1. Translate community needs into a program planning model that can be more easily understood and applied by policy makers, managers, and front line workers.
2. Provide an instrument that can better capture the intangibles of relationships in its evaluations.
3. Bring coherence to social work practice by providing an instrument that recognizes the importance of measuring outcomes of heart and mind, which are the essence of holistic practice.

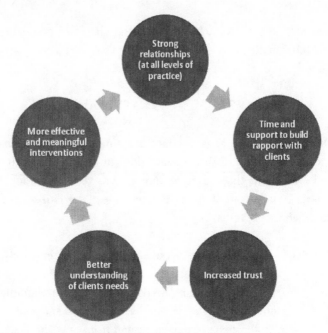

Relationship based practice (diagram 2.)

MODEL OF THE RELATIONAL CHAIN

Current Situation → Proposed Action → Anticipated Outcomes→ Quality Assurance

CURRENT SITUATION

PROBLEM STATEMENT	CURRENT REALITY	OBJECTIVE
Must be succinct and accurate; can be elaborated on in the CURRENT REALITY section.	Sub-text to Problem Statement, elaborates on the issue.	What do we want to achieve?

PROPOSED ACTION

ACTIVITIES What could be done to improve the current situation?	TARGET GROUP Who could benefit from these activities?	RESOURCES What resources would be needed to carry out these activities?

ANTICIPATED OUTCOMES

CLIENT OUTCOMES What will this proposed action do for individuals, families and communities?	SYSTEMIC OUTCOMES What will this proposed action do for the human service system?	ULTIMATE VISION What would it look like in the end?

QUALITY ASSURANCE

WHAT DO YOU WANT TO KNOW • Have you achieved the objective? • What is the impact on clients? • What is the impact on the human services system? • Have you met your ultimate vision?	HOW WILL YOU KNOW IT What information will you require in order to confirm what you want to know?

The Relational Chain (diagram 3)

PRINCIPLES OF THE RELATIONAL CHAIN

- Incorporates relational aspects of human services
- Provides an alternative to the traditional logic model; one that represents the balance of mind and heart in program planning and evaluation, as well as for research proposals by grass roots agencies
- Accessible to all levels of practice; individual practice, management, as well as policy and organizational planning and evaluation.
- Provides the opportunity to evaluate the effectiveness of services based on the context of *relationships* driven by social work values:

Dignity ~ Self-worth ~ Respect ~ Self-determination ~ Acceptance ~ Belonging

- It is easily understood
- It is transferable across organizational boundaries and hierarchies.
- It can inform policy, practice review, and evaluation on an ongoing basis.
- It can enrich personal and professional relationships
- It can create greater understanding between communities, service recipients, service providers, administrators and policy planners.

For the past three decades, the importance of relationship in social work practice and in child welfare has lost ground. We are suggesting that many of today's problems in child welfare practice can be attributed to this loss. We ask if the Relational Chain may not be part of the answer to the problems so often reported, if primary consideration was given to relationships among children, family and community, as well as between the child welfare agency and the people it is mandated to serve.

QUALITY ASSURANCE

We suggest that the Relational Chain is the missing link from many, if not most, quality assurance efforts. The following describes some key features from a quality assurance perspective;

- The Relational Chain assures that the initial intention or purpose is congruent with the impact on the client and the community, by asking:
    - Were the desired outcomes achieved?
    - To what extent?
    - If not, why not?

- The Relational Chain measures and analyzes the contextual conditions that contribute to or negate proposed outcomes. It asks the important questions:
    1.) What do you want to know?
    2.) How will you know it?

CONCLUSION

By focusing on the interaction and relationship between front line workers, children, families, and communities, significant enhancements can be achieved by making more effective use of human and fiscal resources.

The Relational Chain proposes to achieve greater balance between accountability due to government authorities and that due to communities, including those who are served. It brings about not less, but greater accountability, one that is grounded in community responsibility for its children while fully meeting legal accountability to the federal and provincial authorities.

Our ultimate vision is a service system that integrates relational practice and opportunities for reflection to counter balance the overwhelmingly rational system that is currently in place, and to make it more fully human as a result.

REFLECTIONS

1. While this chapter is written in theoretical terms about the interactions between bureaucracies and communities, what parallels can you see in the context of the child protection system and Aboriginal communities?
2. What are the implications for Directors of First Nations agencies who owe an allegiance to the community and local government, whilst being accountable to provincial and federal authorities?
3. How can we ensure that the voice of youth and their families, chiefs and councils, community members and Elders is heard by those who plan and design programs and policies?

SOURCES

Barnard, C. (1938). The Functions of the Executive. Cambridge: Harvard University Press.

Besharov, D. J. (1975). Building a Community Response to Child Abuse and Mistreatment. Children Today, 4, 5.

Elwell. (n.d.). Retrieved July 27, 2006

Gardner, S. L. (1984). Building New Constituencies. Public Welfare, Winter.

Griffiths, S. H. (2000). Reflections on risk in child protection: is it time for a shift in paradigms? *Child and Family Social Work*, 5, 1-10.

Henderson, J.Y. (2000). The context of the state of nature. In M. Battiste (Ed). *Reclaiming indigenous voice and vision.* Vancouver: UBC Press.

Kammerman S. & A. J. Kahn (1989). Social Services for Children, Youth, and Families in the United States. The Annie E. Casey Foundation. Columbia University.

Kweit, M. G. & Kweit, R. W. (1981). Implementing Citizen Participation in a Bureaucratic Society: A Contingency Approach. New York: Praeger Publications

Lafrance, J. & Morris, K. (2008). *The Relational Chain: A Program Planning and Evaluation Model.* Unpublished article.

Lindeman, E. C. (1932). *New Trends in Community Control. Proceedings of the National Conference of Social Work.* Philadelphia, Pennsylvania. May 15-21, 1932. National Conference of Social Work. Chicago: University of Chicago Press.

Litwak, E. & Meyer, H. (1966). A Balance Theory of Coordination between Bureaucratic Organization and Community Primary Groups. <u>Administrative Science Quarterly</u>. (11).

McNair, R. H. et al. (1983). Citizen Participants in Public Bureaucracies: Foul Weather Friends. <u>Administration and Society</u>, <u>14</u>(4), 507-524.

Rappaport, J. (1981). In Praise of Paradox: A Social Policy of Empowerment Over Prevention. <u>American Journal of Community Psychology</u>, <u>9</u>, 1.

Ruch, G. (2005). Relationship-based practice and reflective practice: holistic approaches to contemporary child care social work. *Child and Family Social Work*, *10*, 111-123.

Weinbach, R.W. (1990). <u>The Social Worker as Manager: Theory and Practice</u>. New York: Longman Press.

Winslow, E. (1915). Philanthropic Individualism. <u>*Survey*</u>, <u>34</u>, 555.

Chapter 12

Systemic Racism

Throughout the pages of *Red Brother, White Brother* many topics have been broached, from a brief history to contextual knowledge, from the personal experiences of Aboriginal people and their relationships with the child welfare system to an analysis of the system frameworks in modern day institutions. There is still, however, an important discussion to consider; in order to garner a comprehensive picture of the situation at hand, the larger societal issue of systemic racism must be addressed, as it is at the core of marginalization and inequality.

While there is understandable reluctance to discuss this topic, I hear too many of my Aboriginal friends speak of day-to-day experiences that can only be considered blatant racism. I can only conclude that if this happens to highly educated, professional people, why should we be surprised if it happens to the poor and poorly educated parents of children whose families are so often targeted by the child welfare system?

I cannot help but attribute our lack of success in fundamental change to the existence of a largely racist society. Canadians are known throughout the word as a kind and polite people. We have become more politically correct in our expression, to the extent that most of us are unaware that racism even exists. Lise Noel (cited in Henderson, 2000, p.29) reminds us that systemic colonization is grounded in intolerance. This intolerance comes from unconscious assumptions that underlie "normal institutional rules and collective reactions." It is a consequence of following these rules and accepting these reactions in everyday life that anything or anyone deviating from them is viewed as problematic, as being in need of 'fixing'. These rules, assumptions and reactions are imbedded in the consciousness of all and are so engrained in our day-to-day lives that we do not even realize that they exist. Think for a moment of the analogy of the goldfish in its fishbowl; the goldfish is surrounded by water in its bowl, but yet is completely unaware that it is surrounded by water, or that it is even in a bowl. These realities are a given, are inextricably interwoven into the goldfish's existence, thus making them invisible to the fish altogether. Going back to the accepted assumptions and reactions that have become embedded into our collective consciousness, there is little reason to believe that these attitudes are not deeply engrained in child welfare, just as they are in the rest of Western society.

Young (cited in Henderson, 2000, p.30) poses a conundrum for those who belong to the dominant groups of society:

> *The oppressor has no apparent existence. Not only does he not identify himself as such, but also he is not even supposed to have his own reality. His presence is so immediate and dense and his universe coincides so fully with the Universe that he becomes invisible. Rarely seen, rarely named, he is unique nonetheless and having a full existence as the keeper of the word. He is the supreme programmer who confers various degrees of existence on those who are different from himself . . . as the embodiment of the universal, the dominator is also the only Subject, the Individual, who never being considered to belong*

> *to a particular group can study those impersonal*
> *categories of the population who pose a "problem",*
> *represent a "question", constitute a "case" or simply*
> *have a condition."*

The complexities involved in reconciliation with Aboriginal people by members of the dominant group are no simple matter. We are finding that to support Aboriginal self-determination in the development of policies and practices that are in keeping with Aboriginal traditions and beliefs calls for an uncommon degree of humility and a high degree of receptivity to different ways of thinking. Our challenge is to become consciously aware of how our thoughts and decisions are affected by systemic racism, and to appreciate more thoroughly the challenges encountered by Aboriginal families in dealing with complex institutions like child welfare and the court systems. Each of us needs to look deep into our souls to root out the vestiges of racist attitudes that continue to confound our relationships. This proposal, however, is no easy task; as Carl Jung stated "People will do anything, no matter how absurd, in order to avoid facing their own soul."

So, where do we go from here? I do not have all of the answers. None of us do! However, I believe that between all of us; clients, families, communities, front line staff, administrators, program planners, researchers and academics, policy makers, and politicians, we can come up with a plan.

COLONIZATION IS OVER, ISN'T IT?

When reflecting on colonization, most think of it as an historical event. An event that was not without negative and adverse outcomes, but one of the past, is it not? Yet if one considers current legislations and practices, are they not in keeping with the colonialist attitude of "we" know better than "them?" That Aboriginal people are to adhere to strict Eurocentric ways of living and parenting, and neglecting to do so is at their own peril?

In unpacking this thought, it is important to acknowledge that the prevailing paradigm is that Eurocentric values are preferable, even superior, to others, and not only imposing these values on others but also penalizing them if they do not conform.

> *Federal legislation still considers First Nations people as wards of the government; today's relationship with Indigenous peoples is dominant, one-sided and paternalistic*

If one is still skeptical about the possibility that our systems continue to maintain a racist undertone, consider why there is consistent legislative opposition to handing control of Aboriginal child welfare to Aboriginal communities. Consider why the AANDC (Aboriginal Affairs and Northern Development of Canada, previously known as the Department of Indian Affairs) continues to maintain a dominant, paternalistic relationship with Aboriginal communities. Consider why child protection risk assessments continue to assess families based on Eurocentric values.

As introduced in Chapter 2, seeing the entire 'elephant' is essential to understanding and making changes to the problematic situation at hand. Unless and until these assumptions and beliefs are considered, acknowledged and acted upon, it is unlikely that meaningful change will occur.

> *If we are to break the cycle of destructive practices towards Aboriginal people that has nearly decimated their culture and their way of life, it seems important to reflect on Indigenous peoples' experiences with oppression and colonization over the past 500 years. This calls for an examination of deeply held assumptions, values, and attitudes that can have a sometimes unconscious, but always powerful impact on our behaviors. An alternative perspective is needed that builds greater understanding of the Aboriginal world view.*
> (Bastien & Lafrance, p. 108)

THE ICEBERG METAPHOR

One way to consider the underlying assumptions in our society is through the Iceberg Metaphor.[4]

Often when we look at issues facing Aboriginal communities we design our responses to what is visible, without realizing that there is much more to the problems. There are, in fact, a vast

---

[4] The Iceberg Metaphor was shared by Harley Eagle, a member of the Dakota/Anishinaabe First Nations. He is enrolled in the Wapaha Ska Dakota First Nations Reserve, in Saskatchewan, Canada. Harley works on various programs that address systemic racism, internalized racist oppression and dismantling racism. His contribution here is taken from *Reclaiming and Restoring the Aboriginal Family: Circles of Understanding Curriculum*, Creating Hope Society, 2008

array of systems, relationship, histories, and patterns shaping and supporting each circumstance. In order to address root causes of problems it is vital that we look at the entire picture. Only then can we design programs that not only address immediate needs but also seek to address root problems. What follows is a description of a metaphor to help us understand the structure of the power of racism and the need to go below the surface and address its' foundations. The metaphor is an iceberg divided into three increasingly larger segments as you move down (Figure 1). This figure shows the increasing power that racism has on everyone as you go deeper.

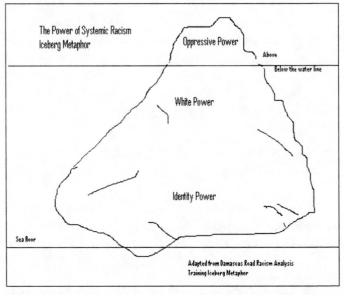

Figure 1—Adapted from Mennonite Central Committee "Damascus Road Racism Analysis Training Process"

The most used definition of racism worldwide is "the systemic misuse of power to enforce racial prejudices," but this description usually only comes up for those that choose to take an analytical look at racism. Commonly, our understanding of racism comes from what we see and hear about in the news in the form of racial hate crimes, police racial profiling, brutality, and overt discriminatory acts based on skin color. We are led to believe that racism is only about acts of brutality performed by ignorant people or bad apples, based on skin color or country of origin. It may also be understood as insensitive things said in the work place or by politicians. These are highly visible, often sensational acts of harm against People of Color (POC). There are usually two ways of dealing with such issues. One is to focus on the bad apples. Get rid of them or train everybody how not to behave badly and to be sensitive to the diversity around them. The second way of dealing with this is to help the POC fit into society around them, don't do anything that draws attention to yourself; be successful in the dominant society to show that you are a good citizen and one who will maintain the status quo therefore will not have these bad things happen to you.

OPPRESSIVE POWER: THE TIP OF THE ICEBERG

Often all we know about racism is that it hurts people of color therefore we design our processes and put our energy into dealing with only this aspect. In terms of the iceberg metaphor we are dealing with only the "tip of the iceberg." For our purposes we call this level "Oppressive Power."

WHITE POWER: INSTITUTIONS AND SYSTEMS

Understanding the next level of the iceberg is often very difficult, this is where we need to put our faces into the cold sea and take a critical and often difficult look at the institutions, and systems around us. Often these systems and institutions are ones that we don't typically spend a lot of time deconstructing; they function as norms in society and we simply interact with them unquestioningly because "that's the way it is."

These are institutions and systems like employment, family, education, and religion. Within the construct of racism and the iceberg as a metaphor we label this level "White Power" and understand that this expresses racism's ability to provide and maintain power and privilege for white people and white society. It is the providing of access and control to institutions, individuals, and systems on the basis of white skin color.

We must be clear that this is the core, the center, the purpose of racism. The core of racism is not intent on hurting POC, it is a result of what is most evident in the whole structure of racism. One could totally eradicate the top level of the iceberg and the core of preserving and maintaining white power and privilege would remain. As mentioned above, this is where we need to critically examine the history of our surroundings, we need to have the courage to face the original intent of institutions and figure out if it is maintained in today's society.

IDENTITY POWER: BELIEFS, ATTITUDES AND ASSUMPTIONS

The third level of the iceberg is the largest, and the deepest. In parallel with its size we say that its power is also the strongest in maintaining the structure of racism. It is here where beliefs are built and maintained, and attitudes are formed, supported, and rewarded. It is therefore the most difficult to understand

and to address. In relation to actual icebergs in the oceans and the damage they can cause beyond sinking ships, the bottom is what drags along the ocean floor and renders it sterile for decades to come. Likewise with our metaphor, this level is the most dangerous; it is labeled Identity Power and shapes the understanding of ourselves.

For folks who are considered white, this is where an identity of superiority is built and maintained. An identity that says our ways are the best and we are the ones that are bringing civilization to the world therefore all people need to believe like us, act like us, talk like us and behave like us and if they don't do so yet, they need to conform. Religious beliefs at this level instills in people that God is on their side and that they are blessed as God's people. For POC at this level an identity that says that "we are inferior" is built and maintained. Our ways are less advanced and our way of doing things is archaic and less important. Our role then becomes one of striving to attain the ways of the white population and their culture, to maintaining their ways, advocating for assimilation, and replacing our traditional teachings, culture and language.

Using the image of an iceberg as metaphor in conjunction with an analysis of racism is extremely helpful in understanding the power that racism actually holds. This in turn helps us shape ways of addressing root causes. In order to dismantle harmful structures we need to broaden our understanding to see racism as a system; we need to examine how it interacts with institutions and people to maintain its power. Using such tools helps us diagnose the visible problems differently and more deeply, getting to the roots of the issue.

WHITE PRIVILEGE: WHAT'S THAT?

In delving into the difficult and painful issues of colonization and assimilation, it is common for those first learning about these issues to respond in a number of ways. One typical response is to say that you had nothing to do with the past, that things are different now and it is time to move forward and forget about what happened. Some will state that decision makers had (and have) the best of intentions, so they really cannot be held at fault—they were only doing what they thought was right. Others will deny having any racist feelings, insisting that they are color blind and treat everyone the same. Yet others will maintain that if you only work hard enough, you can overcome any obstacles and be successful.

All these responses have one thing in common—they are all 'commonsense notions', which means that they are powerful beliefs and comments that have withstood the rigors of time; they have been repeated with such conviction and such frequency that they have become accepted as fact. They are also the social commentaries that reinforce racist ideas and stereotypes.

Why is it necessary to reflect on these ideas and stereotypes? Is it not good enough to just learn about Aboriginal culture, to become 'culturally sensitive' and raise Aboriginal children accordingly? The answer, quite simply, is no. **If we do not question the practices of individuals and institutions, as well as the underlying beliefs that support these practices, then nothing will change.** As previously mentioned, although the sources of authority have changed over time, the outcomes for Aboriginal children overwhelmingly continue to be the same. Children are still experiencing loss of community connections, loss of identity and sense of belonging, and loss of hope for the future. What we have right now is the continuation of a cycle, and it is a cycle that does not produce good outcomes for the children and families involved.

At this point many express feelings of defensiveness; after all, not one of us is personally responsible for the system as it is. You may want to resist this train of thought, or insist that it does not apply to you. These reactions are common and very normal; when we are questioned about what we believe, about the world that we live in, this causes discomfort. We encourage you, however, to stay with us before choosing to turn away. We invite you to participate in an exercise that will challenge you to dig deeper and ask yourself "how do we, as a society, support these ideas and stereotypes, without even realizing that we are doing so?"

> *Ccommonsense notions are powerful beliefs and comments that have withstood the rigors of time; they have been repeated with such conviction and such frequency that they have become accepted as fact.*

EXERCISE: MAKING VISIBLE THE INVISIBILITY OF WHITE PRIVILEGE[5]

This exercise helps to uncover the invisibility of privilege that white people experience in their day to day lives. We invite you,

---

[5]   Adapted from "Unpacking the Invisible Backpack" by Peggy McIntosh, 1989.

whoever you are, to fill out this checklist and think about how you do or do not experience any of these privileges.

Check each box that applies to you.

☐ I can, if I wish, arrange to be in the company of people of my race most of the time.

☐ If I should need to move, I can be pretty sure of renting or purchasing housing in an area that I can afford and in which I would want to live.

☐ I can be pretty sure that my neighbors in such a location will be neutral or pleasant to me.

☐ I can go shopping alone most of the time, pretty well assured that I will not be followed or harassed.

☐ I can turn on the television or open to the front page of the paper and see people of my race widely represented.

☐ When I am told about our country's history or about "civilization," I am shown that people of my color made it what it is.

☐ I can be sure that my children will be given school materials that testify to the existence of their race.

☐ I can go to a music shop and count on finding the music of my race represented, into a supermarket and find the staple foods that fit with my cultural traditions, into a hairdresser's shop and find someone who can deal with my hair.

☐ Whether I use cheques, credit cards, or cash, I can count on my skin color not to work against the appearance of financial reliability.

☐ I can arrange to protect my children most of the time from people who might not like them.

☐ I do not have to educate my children to be aware of systemic racism for their own daily physical protection.

☐ I can swear, or dress in second hand clothes or not answer letters without having people attribute these choices to the bad morals, the poverty, or the illiteracy of my race.

☐ I can speak in public to a powerful male group without putting my race on trial.

☐ I can do well in a challenging situation without being called a credit to my race.

☐ I am never asked to speak for all the people of my racial group

☐ I can remain oblivious of the language and customs of persons of color, who constitute the worlds' majority, without feeling in my culture any penalty for such oblivion.

☐ I can criticize our government and talk about how much I fear its policies and behavior without being seen as a cultural outsider.

☐ I can be sure that if I ask to talk to "the person in charge," I will be facing a person of my race.

☐ If a traffic cop pulls me over, or if the government audits my tax return, I can be sure I haven't been singled out because of my race.

☐ I can easily buy posters, postcards, picture books, greeting cards, dolls, toys, and children's magazines featuring people of my race.

☐ I can go home from most meetings or organizations I belong to feeling somewhat tied in rather than isolated, out of place, outnumbered, held at a distance, or feared.

- ☐ I can take a job with an affirmative action employer without having co-workers on the job suspect that I got it because of my race.
- ☐ I can choose public accommodation without fearing that people of my race cannot get in or will be mistreated in the places I have chosen.
- ☐ I can be sure that if I need legal or medical help my race will not work against me.
- ☐ If my day, week, or year is going badly, I need not ask of each negative episode or situation whether it has racial overtones.
- ☐ I can choose blemish cover or bandages in "flesh" color that more or less matches my skin.

Summary

The point of this exercise is to uncover the invisibility of the advantages given to some people and not to others. It is also to dispel the myth that racism is only found in individual acts of meanness or dominance by certain people or certain groups. Whether you look for it or not, you receive certain social advantages (or privileges) when you belong to the dominant group; this is what we call white privilege, or invisible privilege.

REFLECTIONS

1. How did you feel when answering these questions?
2. Were you surprised by any of these questions or answers? Were they questions that you have asked yourself in the past, or are they things that you just take for granted in your life?
3. Did this exercise help you to see how those from the 'dominant group' could easily take for granted the privileges that they receive, just for the color of their skin?

SOURCES

Bastien, B. and Lafrance, J. (2007). Here be dragons! Reconciling Indigenous and western knowledge to improve Aboriginal child welfare. *First Peoples Child & Family Review*, 3(1), pp.105-126.

Henderson, J.Y. (2000). The context of the state of nature. In M. Battiste (Ed). *Reclaiming indigenous voice and vision*. Vancouver: UBC Press.

PART IV

Merging the Experience of Aboriginal People with Program and Policy Change

~ THE MOST PROMISING SURVIVAL PATH FOR
HUMANS IS TO MERGE EXISTING TECHNOLOGY
WITH THE KNOWLEDGE, WISDOM, AND
ECOLOGICALLY SOUND PRACTICE OF INDIGENOUS
AND TRADITIONAL PEOPLES ~

(SAHTOURIS, 1992, P.1).

Chapter 13

Towards Healing and Reconciliation

It is clear from conversations with Aboriginal people that they have placed much of their hope for change in a return to traditional values.

> *Those communities who have had the most success in dealing with the psychological legacy of colonialism are those that have found a way to operate within their cultural context and drawing on . . . the spiritual and other strengths that are present in their culture."*

> *(A speaker at the Royal Commission*
> *|on Aboriginal Peoples; 1994; 48)*

In recent years, Aboriginal people have resolved to overcome the pain and loss that are the legacy of colonization through healing, reconciliation, and self-determination (Aboriginal Healing Foundation, 2005; Berry and Brink, 2004). A major part of healing and reconciliation is building on the strengths and resilience of Aboriginal people and reclaiming Aboriginal culture, identity, and pride (Aboriginal Healing Foundation, 2005; Berry and Brink, 2004). Indeed, Aboriginal people are mobilizing to recover from the trauma and oppression of residential schools and genocide, and revitalizing their language, customs, spirituality, traditions, values and beliefs

(York, 1990). York (1990) concludes that today, "evidence of a cultural revival can be seen across Canada . . . [It] is just one step toward regaining what has been lost" (p. 264, 269).

REVIVAL AND PRESERVATION OF LANGUAGE

The promotion and preservation of Aboriginal languages is a crucial part of the healing, renewal and rebirth of Aboriginal people (Royal Commission on Aboriginal Peoples, 1994). Language is an expression of the culture and a reflection of the identity of the people, derived of shared experiences, values, feelings, ideas and worldviews (Boldt, 1993; York, 1990). Language is particularly important in Aboriginal culture because of the role of oral tradition in the transmission of cultural values, ways of living, and life philosophies (Boldt, 1993). The Assembly of First Nations (AFN) has argued that language is the cornerstone of Aboriginal people, emphasizing its importance in Aboriginal culture, spirituality and traditions and in the survival of the people (Royal Commission on Aboriginal Peoples 1994; 45). Boldt (1993) concludes that "when a language dies, the world-view is lost . . . Only through their indigenous languages can today's Indians fully access the knowledge, wisdom, sentiments, and meanings offered by their cultural heritage" (p. 187). In short, the survival of Indigenous languages is critical to the healing and revitalization of Aboriginal people and culture.

ATONEMENT: BEING OF ONE MIND

The common modern day definition of the word 'atonement' is to make amends or reparation for an injury or wrong. If one looks deeper, however, there is another meaning to the word that is very relevant to this discussion.

The word atonement breaks down into at-one-ment. Language history tells us that this term comes from one of two Latin words. The first is a derivation of the Latin word *adunare*, meaning to unite or make as one. The second possibility is from the Latin word *reconciliation*, meaning to bring together again, to restore to union.

This calls us to a meeting of minds between dominant child welfare systems and Aboriginal culture, tradition, and spirituality. An examination of the historical context of Aboriginal and non-Aboriginal relations can help us to better understand why bringing both groups together is essential to address the impact of child welfare systems upon Aboriginal communities, families and children.

The following strategies may serve as a starting point to get into the water, to the level of our knees, and not too far from shore, for those of us who are faint-hearted or dubious of the need to dive into "new waters":

- Bottom up or backward mapping; starts with people and works backward to tell officials what social policies or programs are necessary. One study in the central region of Alberta reminded us that what is most important to families is a relationship with the social worker who respects their dignity and individuality, provides for self-determination, and allows for a holistic and flexible approach to solving their problems.

- Focus on the creation of new settings of mutual aid and informal supports for people who are isolated or who are trapped in harmful settings.
- Encourage shared decision-making, participatory planning and problem solving, and mutual interdependence.
- Increase opportunities for client and staff participation in decision-making. In the words of one social worker:

  We need an organizational culture in which staff are free to examine their practice . . . we need to create an environment where reflective learning from clients and consumer groups can become a standard part of practice . . .

- Create fluid roles for staff rather than ones that are rigidly defined. One participant in our study represented the views of many when she stated:

  It opened up the door with workers to be more creative with their clients . . . we need to have more leeway in the services we provide to families, because they don't fit the categories. Sometimes we have to do something special and we need the freedom to do that.

- Structure conflict so it will be constructive rather than destructive.
- Create a Dionysian ideology that focuses on purpose and mission as opposed to an Apollonian ideology that is overly focused upon self-preservation.

- Engage in phenomenological research—discover how clients experience our programs and incorporate this information into program design. According to a casework supervisor in Alberta:

    Well, I think we do need to look at practice in light of feedback from clients, and it's been hard for us to do at this point in time because we've not had an effective way of getting information back from clients . . . to ask "do these policies and procedures make sense from their perspective?" They might make sense in terms of accountability in the system, having back-ups for decision-making, they may help the system run a little more smoothly, but do they in fact help us to be (more) effective?

- Place the questions that concern us in the larger historical and normative context in which they reside.
- Develop a boundary spanning management style, which assists staff and clients to discover and pursue their own developmental needs, even if these might potentially conflict with bureaucratic imperatives.
- Find ways for clients to direct their own destiny and collaborate with them as peers.

We need to keep in mind that we can best ensure success by becoming aware of the influence of prevailing paradigms upon our practice. Rappaport (1981) proposes that there is no one best way to solve the problems that face us, but that there are many divergent ways available to communities, service providers, and academics.

The difficulty involved with change cannot be under-estimated, but each of us can illustrate the possibility. It only requires that we step out of expected and typical institutional relationships to find a common ground of caring, respect, and flexibility, along with an orientation toward action from a research and an educational perspective. The community, policy makers, and academia can work together to merge knowledge from "mainstream" theory, practice, and research pertaining to children's services with the traditional wisdom of First Nations communities. It requires for us to drop the barriers that keep us apart. It is a path that calls on each of us to better understand the other's view of reality, as we find ways to solve problems that would be unmanageable on our own. By creating a convergence of our two rivers, Aboriginal and "mainstream" for lack of a more descriptive term, is it not possible to create new knowledge that would not only better serve Aboriginal communities, but ultimately all communities? To achieve this vision I call for the deepening of a concerted effort between provincial authorities and Aboriginal people to ensure that the destructive federal fiscal policy that has been in place for over a century is rescinded and replaced by one that does not result in the continuing removal of children from their families and communities. It promotes a deeper understanding of the contribution of Aboriginal spirituality to a more holistic and community centered practice model. It calls on us to develop a deeper understanding of the oppression inflicted on Aboriginal people and the outcomes that continue to plague them today, and to be fully attentive to the perspectives of Aboriginal communities. Thus we may be able to weave a new tapestry created from our shared wisdom.

SOURCES

Boldt, M. (1993). *Surviving as Indians: The challenge of self-government.* Toronto, ON: University of Toronto Press.

York, G. (1990). *The dispossessed: Life and death in Native Canada.* London: Vintage U.K.

Rappaport, J. (1981). In Praise of Paradox: A Social Policy of Empowerment Over Prevention. <u>American Journal of Community Psychology</u>, 9, 1.

RCAP. Royal Commission on Aboriginal Peoples. (1994). Available from <u>http://www.ainc-inac.gc.ca/ch/rcap/sg/ci2_e.pdf</u>

Sahtouris, E. (1992). *The survival path: Cooperation between indigenous and industrial humanity.* Proceedings of the United Nations Policy Meeting on Indigenous Peoples. Santiago, Chile. Available at www.<u>http://www.ratical.com/LifeWeb/Articles/survival.html</u>.

CHILD WELFARE POLICY ANALYSIS

This policy analysis paper was prepared by Amber Dion, a First Nations student at the Blue Quills MSW program as a part of her Social Policy course requirements. It addresses so many important issues with such passion and credibility that I asked for her permission to include it in this work. I am grateful that Amber has agreed to do so, and thank her for her contribution.

Her presence, along with her many colleagues who are following graduate studies with the Calgary Faculty of Social Work, give me hope for the future of Aboriginal people and our ability to work together.

Policy problem

Currently, provincial and delegated First Nations children's services authorities are mandating parents and youth to attend drug and alcohol treatment programs through court orders. Many families who are involved with the child welfare system are forced to do this in order to get their children back into their care after apprehension and temporary guardianship has been granted. Youth who are also involved with the system are being forced to attend treatment programs in order to be re connected with their families or communities.

It is my understanding that the goals and objectives of this policy is to encourage healthier lifestyles for families and communities. With children's safety as the priority, child welfare mandates this policy to protect children from drug, alcohol and substance abuse exposure and trauma associated with addictions. While this policy has children's best interest at heart, I believe it fails to consider the emotional, mental, spiritual and physical needs of the parent(s) who are having difficulty with drugs, alcohol and other substances.

During his presentation "The Awasis Story," Gerard Bellefeuille spoke about the authority social workers, more specifically child welfare workers, are given by the government. Police officers and other enforcement do not have the power to walk into your home and apprehend your children, but child welfare workers can do that based upon allegations, screenings and investigations of reported abuse. In this context, one person essentially has the power to dictate the lives of grandparents, parents and children. Furthermore, the role of the child welfare worker impacts systems within the community including leadership and other social programs. The decisions made by the child welfare worker also affect how systems work together or how they do not work together. The intrusive policies, procedures and protocols of the child welfare system have been observed and felt negatively for many years in First Nations communities, even by those who are not "directly" affected by the system.

In my experience, I have considered myself as an outsider, looking in; I have not been employed as a child welfare worker, but I have worked with children, parents and grandparents who are involved with the system. The hundreds of stories that people have shared with me regarding their experiences with loss, grief, identity, addictions, poverty, voicelessness, powerlessness, and fear has impacted who I am, not just as a social worker, but as a human being. Their stories are why I feel passionate about this policy that provincial and delegated First

Nations authorities have put into place to force people to get treatment for alcohol and drugs.

While I intuitively understand the implementation of referring people to get help with addictions, I disagree with the conceptualization of the policy. In my current work, our program is assisting 40 families identify and secure supports and resources to develop life skills, parenting skills and to make healthier lifestyle choices. Approximately half of these families are currently involved with child welfare, or have history with child welfare. At our office, we see parent's frustration of "jumping through the child welfare hoops", one of which is completion of drug/alcohol treatment programs. During my first year of the social work diploma program, I heard the statement, "we can't force people to change" regularly in class. That has always stayed with me, and I have defiantly learned that it is true in both my personal and professional experience. What surprises me is that social workers, after learning about human behavior, abuse, and family systems, are still trying to force change through programming and policies. What I believe we have done is made our jobs a lot harder and set ourselves up for disappointment in many ways by looking at our families and communities from a deficit perspective.

A very important piece in understanding addiction is understanding history, more specifically family history. Colonization and residential schools impacted First Nations communities nationwide; inter-generational effects are still impacting our communities today. Dr. Leona Makokis (2005) describes the removal of First Nations children from their homes then being forcibly placed in residential school as "legalized kidnapping" (p. 3). We, as Indigenous people, have experienced undeniable trauma at the hands of others during colonization. Now, with our current child welfare system, we are practicing internal oppression through apprehending children from their homes and placing them in foreign group homes and communities. Historical trauma and continuous repeated trauma is affecting our parenting skills, relationships, boundaries, and our lifestyle choices. So, how do we cope with all this accumulated pain, loss and grief? To connect trauma and addiction, Tian Dayton (2000) states that, "providing short term aid for underlying emotional pain that remains unchanged or can sometimes worsen due to the lack of processing the pain that can lead to self-medication and addiction" (p. 20).

According to Dr. Gabor Mate, who has extensively researched addictions at the neurobiological level, overcoming an addiction is much more complex than most professionals understand. I believe that defining addiction is very difficult due to the personalization of feelings and effects on an individual; what I identify as an addiction may not be what others feel is an addiction. Mate's definition of addiction is, "any repeated behavior, substance-related or not, in which a person feels compelled to persist, regardless of its negative impact on his life and the lives of others" (Mate, 2008, p. 214). He suggests that we, as addicts, do not have choice in "feeding" our addictions due to infant and childhood brain development where patterns and reactions to stress are pre-determined. "All addictions engage the brain's attachment-reward and incentive-motivation systems, which, in turn, escape from the regulation by the "thinking" and impulse control areas of the cortex" (Mate, 2008, p. 215). Mate (2008) describes the three dominant brain systems in addiction as the opioid attachment-reward system, the dopamine-based incentive-motivation apparatus and the self-regulation areas of the prefrontal cortex (p.188). These vital systems can be altered negatively during childhood and without treatment, can affect responses that can lead to addictive behavior. The brain is a multifaceted organ which sends thousands of signals to the rest of our body each day.

Dr. Bruce Perry, who also specializes in trauma and brain development, describes the basic functions of each part of the brain; there are four parts that have different responsibilities. Although these parts have separate functions, they also are very connected during a response or transmission of a message. Perry (2006) states that when a child experiences a trauma, whether it is a onetime occurrence or repeated, it can have devastating effects on the way in which messages are transmitted; therefore, affect the reaction to future stress (p. 6). Abnormal or low functioning systems within the brain may influence how children play with other children, how well they do in school, and their ability to cope. His worldview can also be used to explain why we cope with stress through use of addictions.

After exploring historical trauma, inter-generational trauma, effects of trauma on brain development, how trauma induced brain damage affects our coping skills and reactions to stress, and the complexity of the addiction process, is it reasonable for social workers to give a parent three months to get sober, develop a clean healthy lifestyle, and to heal all their wounds?

I believe that it is an ineffective practice, causing more damage to families by setting unrealistic goals, not with, but for parents and their children. When I need a reminder of how difficult it really is to begin a healing journey and stop feeding into addictions, I think of my father who is a residential school survivor and was an alcoholic for many, many years. He attended 28 treatment programs before he quit drinking, many of which were court ordered due to criminal charges. My dad always says, "There is a difference between healing and sobering up, I can be sober but still very wounded. I had to start healing to keep sober and change my life."

By mandating parents and children involved in the child welfare system to attend treatment programs, social workers are implying, sometimes directly, that they have one chance to change everything in 28 days or they don't get their kids back. If treatment is not completed, the client is deemed as non-compliant with the service plan and is penalized. I have witnessed social workers refusing parents visits or other forms of contact with their children because they have not completed treatment, therapy, anger management, or drug testing. I have also seen children return to their home very soon after a parent completes treatment, giving the parent and children very limited time to adjust to their new lifestyle. According to my community's NNADAP director, more than half of the referrals they send off to treatment are court ordered by child welfare, and very few actually complete treatment. That reality is saddening for parents, children, extended families and community.

Key stakeholders

Who is going to be mad about this policy? The parents and youth who are forced to attend treatment programs, most of which are long distances from their home communities, would be angry. In Alberta, there are six NNADAP adult treatment centers spread across the province. For someone from my home community, Kehewin Cree Nation, the closest center is Beaver Lake Wah Pow, which is approximately a 1 ½ hour drive. Transportation is an issue in many First Nations communities and our NNADAP workers are not responsible for any transportation for clients and their families. In addition to the stress of leaving their home community, people attending treatment fear what will happen next (fear of the unknown). As I discussed earlier, the complexity of addiction itself and the brain's patterns would cause confusion and frustration, both of which are associated with anger.

Who is going to be glad about this policy? Child welfare workers would benefit from their clients attending treatment, as this would mean people moving towards healing and getting their children back into their care. The children and families would also directly benefit from their loved ones receiving treatment for addictions. Healthy choices, relationships and lifestyles affect children's quality of life and facilitate healthy brain development. Furthermore, positive role modeling encourages children to make good choices in childhood through to adulthood. Community agencies such as social development, health services, NNADAP, and economic development would also benefit from this policy. The more families receiving addictions treatment and on the recovery road would lessen caseloads and create a healthier community. Of course, this would all depend solely on whether or not a client successfully completes treatment and continues to make healthy choices.

Who is going to be sad about this policy? Parents and youth attending treatment programs may experience sadness for a variety of reasons. As mentioned before, leaving their home community, family and friends creates sadness. I have also heard clients in a treatment center say that giving up their addiction, lifestyle, and the circle of friends who also participate in that lifestyle creates sadness. Regardless of context and personal situation, any change will bring about different emotions depending on coping skills. The families of people leaving for extended periods of time would also be affected. As noted earlier, the chances of court ordered clients completing treatment are slim. Families and children who are hopeful that their loved ones are going to get the help they need to change unhealthy lifestyles would be directly affected and saddened.

Alternative solutions

The objective and goal of the current policy is to encourage healthier lifestyles, families and communities by forcibly sending some parents and youth involved in the child welfare system to addictions treatment programs. With stressful time constraints, tremendous pressure from child welfare and complex addiction processes all working against families, the policy in debate is simply not effective.

I suggest three alternatives that would still encourage healthier lifestyles, relationships and communities. First, I believe it is vital to give parents and youth voice in goal setting and treatment options. When a family is broken due to addictions issues, child welfare should be creating open, honest dialogue with families about their wants, needs and wishes. Trusting relationships between child welfare and families would also need to be created in order for this type of empowering practice to take place. Family group conferencing, where immediate and extended family is involved, is a holistic tool that facilitates healing, and should be utilized during every family plan. During treatment plans, the family can decide where the children are placed while they complete treatment. By using this method, stress will be reduced, therefore; allowing parents or youth to focus on their emotional, mental, physical and spiritual needs. Furthermore, families need to identify their addictions, where they feel they need help, and how that would look. Far too often, child welfare workers identify their client's problems and tell them what they need, which creates additional resistance and fear of judgment.

Second, parents and children need to stay connected while involved with the child welfare system. Consistent, predictable, structured visits should be maintained with families during involvement and in this context while parents or youth are in treatment. As a parent, I cannot imagine not seeing my daughter for weeks or months at a time. I believe it is important for not just children, but also for parents to have regular visitation and phone contact to prevent further trauma. I also believe that all parents love their children and vice versa, regardless of negative history; child welfare needs to honor that unconditional love by protecting visitation and contact. I understand that in many cases it is the parents who do not follow through with visits; this goes back to building healthy, trusting relationships with child welfare workers. By keeping family connections alive, parents and children have something to look forward to and something to be proud of. I recall a story from a past client who was in treatment: he said that the only thing keeping him in treatment was seeing his daughters every week. A driver would bring his children to the treatment center once a week and they had an opportunity to spend quality time together as a family. The hope and dreams of what the future held outside of treatment is what kept him going, and that is what is important.

Third, clients who do not complete treatment should not be reprimanded with such serious consequences. While I understand the need for accountability, the penalties for non-compliance are often very traumatic. Also, families should be given more flexibility with timeframes. I believe it is very unfair to ask someone who has struggled with an addiction for 20 years to "fix" their problems within three or six months. I have witnessed child welfare request a lengthy to do list for families including finding safe, secure housing, complete treatment, attend therapy, complete random drug testing, end an abusive relationship, and to get involved with other community programs. A list of that nature is very overwhelming, especially with a timeframe of six months. If children's services were able to create more flexible practices while still keeping children's safety as a priority, families would succeed. The saying, "No one wins when everyone is losing" would be appropriate when discussing rigid policies preventing children and parents from being together. Instead of parents or youth being threatened with a permanent guardianship order or refusal of visits, options should be explored with families about next steps. Consequences should also be identified by families to create accountability, meaning and personal commitment.

Assessment of alternatives

From a child welfare perspective, the priority is the safety and wellbeing of the child, which I believe leaves parents voiceless and powerless. My suggestions for alternative practice is family and community based, including grandparents, parents, friends, cousins, informal family supports, community agencies and resources, and leadership. With the implementation of all policies, there are going to be people who are sad, people who are mad, and people who are glad. The suggestions I have made would create the same reactions with all stakeholders.

Child welfare may not consider implementing the family group conferencing tool due to lack of family involvement with a case, or lack of "positive" family members who can contribute to the process. I believe that many families and child welfare workers do not use this holistic approach because power is no longer in the hands of one person; the entire group holds the power in this context. First Nations people have normalized dependency on authority figures to make decisions for entire communities and families. Moreover, the fear of having a voice and being involved in important decision making can cause resistance.

Keeping family connections through visits and other contact may not be an option for many families due to child safety issues. In my experience I have heard child welfare workers say that there is too high of risk for a child to visit his family due to sexual abuse or violence. By asking the child to visit with a perpetrator may cause additional trauma. It is my belief that regardless of what is going on with a family, the child needs to stay connected with someone in their community. A child may identify a support as a teacher or a friend's parent; ensuring children have something to hang on to is so crucial to their wellbeing.

Child welfare has strict policies in place to secure children's safety, and giving timelines for parents to complete tasks is one of those rigid policies. There is a stigma associated with parents who have had their children apprehended, and that is they should be doing everything child welfare tells them to do to get their kids back; if they don't, it proves they don't love their kids. We, as communities, need to eliminate these stigmas to alleviate the guilt and shame our families are already feeling to support healthy choices and relationships. Child welfare authorities do have mandated policies that they must follow to ensure children are safe, and I believe that prevents many workers to be flexible. I also believe this has a lot to do with training and awareness; if social workers had a better understanding of history, it may be that perspectives would shift.

Barriers to implementation

The barriers for implementing a holistic, family based approach to treatment and family planning are:

- the current child welfare policies
- child welfare workers perspectives, practices models, and training
- the community stakeholders (other social programs and leadership and community members at large)
- families' perspectives, self-efficacy, self-esteem, and confidence
- government policies and programming, and current bureaucracy
- differences in worldviews (holistic verses western)
- funding limitations

I believe that change is already happening, slowly, in many of our communities. The families, who are the key stakeholders, need to begin voicing their concerns and opinions, but they also need someone who will listen.

Recommendations

Our community leadership plays a huge role in decision making process in many capacities. I believe that they would need to be at the table with child welfare and families discussing what has been done, and what needs to be done. We often seek answers from our leadership when really those answers are within ourselves. Also, networking with other community agencies, meeting with each other to avoid duplication of services, and supporting one another in assisting families is vital to building healthy communities. We need to be taking every opportunity possible for hearing the voices of our families; what are their needs, their wishes and dreams. Most importantly, we need community wide healing, not just for our families who are involved in the child welfare system.

I remember the quote, "I met the enemy, and the enemy is us". I believe as social workers we need to be reminded that our power should not be something we use to oppress others but instead to advocate for others. In a presentation from Willie Ermine (2009), he asked the question, "When you work in your communities, ask yourself, what system am I feeding?" When child welfare workers forcibly send parents and youth to treatment programs when they are not ready for it, what system are we feeding? When families are falling apart in our communities and we continue to support that by apprehending children, what system are we feeding? When we disconnect parents and children from everything they know and love, what system are we feeding? My answer is that we are feeding the wrong system: the system of oppression, colonization, dysfunction, and sadness.

My dream is healthy communities and healthy families, and I will feed the system that encourages those dreams.

"By the group they were wounded, by the group
they shall be healed"

J.L. Moreno

REFERENCES

Bellefeuille, G. (2009). *In class instruction.* SOWK 665: Blue
Quills First Nations College.

Dayton, T. (2000). *Trauma and Addiction.* Florida: Health
Communications, Inc.

Dion, G. (1998). *Oral Teachings:* Kehewin Cree Nation.

Makokis, L. (2005). *A Residential School Narrative.* SW 667:
Blue Quills First Nations College.

Mate, G. (2008). *In the Realm of Hungry Ghosts.* Toronto:
Vintage Canada.

Perry, B.D. (2006). *The Boy Who Was Raised as a Dog.* New
York: Basic Books.

CPSIA information can be obtained at www.ICGtesting.com
Printed in the USA
LVOW131932110213

319628LV00002B/3/P